Flow

Paul Hodgon

Flow

Copyright © 2016 Paul Hodgon

All rights reserved.

ISBN-13: 978-1539475989

ISBN-10: 1539475980

DEDICATION

To all those I've met in life's journey.
To my wonderful children Claire & Rob who put up with a different Dad.
To Isaac, welcome to the world, Grandson.
Finally To Rose whose wanderings I crossed many times over the last 25 years never dreaming that after many years of supporting each other as friends we would finally be seeing out the last years of our spiritual and physical lives together.

Flow

CONTENTS

	Acknowledgments	i
1	Introduction	1
2	Chalice	Pg 3
3	Prelude	Pg 67
4	Water of Life	Pg 76
5	Prelude	Pg 156
6	Origins	Pg 160
7	Ahma's Labyrinthine Child	Pg 166
8	Afterword	Pg 220
9	Canticles	Pg 228
10	Index to Chalice	Pg 251
11	Notes	Pg 252

Flow

Flow

ACKNOWLEDGEMENTS

Edmund Spenser for the Spenserian stanza used in the Fairie Queen which I have used later in the book. Brothers Grimm for the Water of life which I have added to and written the prequels and sequels. Influential in the themes have been so many writers in the Western Mystery Traditions read over the past 40 plus years including WG Gray, RJ Stewart, Anastacia Nutt, Paracelsus, A.E. Waite, Ross Nichols, Alan Richardson, Gareth Knight, Dion Fortune, St. Francis, St Theresa of Avila, St. John of the Cross, Mabinogion, Kathleen Raine, William Blake, Rudyard Kipling and Madame Porette. Though nothing has been used directly from their works the poems and prose do reflect many of the themes therein. The cover was inspired by RJ Stewart's 'The Arch of Heaven'. Some of the Canticles were particularly inspired by the work and teachings of OBOD, RJ Stewart, Anastacia Nutt. Father Silhouan and me.

Flow

Introduction

Flow is a collection of poetry and prose focused on themes of the Western mystical traditions which begin in prehistory and continue through Pythagoras, Plato, Judaism, Druidry, Christianity and much more.

The first collection: Chalice contains meditations, visions and reflections set out in both poetry and prose. Here the foundation is laid for the later ballads. Sometimes there is one short poem or thought on a page. This is so personal notes and reflections can be added. Some continually lead the reader to a single word which is the point, or points, of that poem. Too often we race through life and rarely pause to reflect. In these arhythmic and sometimes shape poems the emphasis is reflection on the whole concept with some focus on a single word. Here even the word 'and' can be significant.

The ballad and its preludes springboards off The Water of Life in the Brothers Grimm collection of fairy tales. In the ballads, using Spenserian stanzas, the concepts of Chalice are brought to life in a fantasy style setting involving the underworld of Faerie and Ancestors, On world or human realm and the Divine realm. Some find the ballad challenging to read due to its use of convoluted syntax and little use of articles. Other readers are caught by the rhythm of the meter so this ceases to be an issue as the convoluted syntax ceases to be noticed.

In Ahma's Labrynthine Child I have extended Spenser's classic stanza. The poems are written using the Spenserian stanza as a basis. However, from 'Origins' onwards I have decided to reinforce the concepts which underpin the second two poems by extending the use of the Alexandrine hexameter of the 9th line.
I have called this the Extended Spenserian stanza form.
The stanzas are set in an 18 stanza pattern. The aim of the new form was to emphasise a sense of rising to a zenith then descending as in a lunar or solar cycle. The 1st and 18th are regular Spenserian stanzas. But then to underpin the concept of breathing in and out and the waxing and waning of the moon an Alexandrine rises through lines 8,6,4,2 then 7,5,3, 1 then descends in reverse so 1,3,5,7 and 2,4,6,8.

The ascending and descending is emphasised by the left/right formatting which seeks also to emulate the sunwise motion of the northern hemisphere. This, hopefully, will also reinforce the energies expended and themes in each 18 stanza set. This also plays with numbers as in numerology the 18 leads to 8 + 1 =9, 9 reduces to 3 and 3 to 1 and 1 to 0 which links the themes to the Western Tree of Life concepts of All and Naught, the Laws of life and death and western wheel of life.

Much of the ballads imagery has been drawn from British and Greek mythology and the obscure writings in alchemical books such as The Hermetic Museum, the writings of Paracelsus, Giordano Bruno, Robert Fludd,others and 58 years of spiritual experiences and dreams.

FOREWORD:

CHALICE

These are shape poems, meditations and reflections shared with some small
groups or friends over the last 45 years.
They are not answers, they are more responses, to life
and the desire to become a better
expression of being brought into
expression with the gift of life
and the desire to maximise the
freedom of the soul and spirit
to connect to their unmanifest source,
which brought into being
two streams, knowing
that in the creation of manifestation
would come
choice.
Some
would use
choice
to focus on
the manifest world and
starve their
soul and spirit
of connection to the source.

Flow

Do not look for the answers here but look rather
for the 'shorter way' as the Mystics call it.
There is magic here but not of the
controlling type. Reflections are focused
on transforming
expression
into connection by
allowing soul
and spirit
freedom
to
connect.
Don't dither, dally or
delay there's work to be done.

Small Learnings Pre 2011

Ten Thoughts

Thought 1
On Standing
(A response to WG Gray's comments on Standing written many years before I read it)

A time is coming when many must be strong and brave
honour well.
Help always comes from unexpected places.
Don't use sight as looks deceive the eyes of the needy.
Learn well

This will not be the time for faint hearts and weariness.
Sleep will be a luxury
Learn to sleep awake.
Fear only to the level which is sensible.
The night cannot harm you
-only that which hides in it.

Here, smell, sense well,
trust instinct,
stay silent,
Learn to hold your silence ,
filter the aches.
Concentrate on your blood flow.
Survive you can if you learn well.
Learn to leave no tracks.
Daylight will come and
troubles cease,
live for the dawn.
Savour the journey and Live well.
Life is the Treasure
Love is the Carrier
Morning comes
See her Star

Thought 2
On Guardianship

Beware Merchants of Doom.
They prey on your fear,
they feed off it,
from this they draw power and become
elevated.
Trust none who stand above others on platforms
to be seen and heard
Trust none who set themselves apart.
Trust none who claim to stand between Maker and Made.

All are welcome,
none are discarded.

Wear not your suffering like medals,
this insults those who truly
Suffer.

Judge none,
everyone has Their Story,
let them judge themselves.
Walk Quietly,
Peacefully,
leave no tracks.

Life is the Treasure
Love is the Carrier
Morning comes
See Her Star

Thought 3
On Empathy

Empathise,
but don't say you've been there.
You haven't,
you've been to your own place,
it is not the same place as the place of others.

You don't have their fears,
anxieties, history of highs and lows,
joys and tears.
You don't have their History,
their perspectives,
their precise Worldsight,
their perspectives.
You cannot Know,
but,
you can show Empathy, Love, Life
and share their Hope.
Life is the treasure
Love is the Carrier
Morning comes
See Her Star

Thought 4
on the Treasure

Give freely, share all,
but,
Be Wise,
For some the final sacrifice is right,
but not for all.
Life is the Treasure
Love is the Carrier
Morning comes
See her Star.
Don't precipitate unnecessarily your crossing
into the realms beyond before your time.
Bitter ghosts will not help the living.

Life is the Treasure
Love is the Carrier
Morning comes
See Her Star.

Thought 5
On Talk

Small talk can become a consuming Fire of
misunderstanding
which none know whence it came.
Learn Well to Control It.
Guard your tongue,
Learn Well to Control it.
Anger is a double edged sword which invariably
cuts
its bearer.

Life is the Treasure
Love is the Carrier
Morning comes
See Her Star

Thought 6
On Jesus Said

Do You Love Your Self?
To love others as You Love Yourself
is impossible
if You
don't
love yourself.
Think...
do you do to yourself
that which you wouldn't do
to others?
Do you treat as yourself
as you would
never dream
of treating others?
Hard isn't it?
Maybe
Life is the Treasure
Love is the Carrier
Morning comes
See Her Star

Thought 7
On Time

When you master Time it will be your helper forever.
In order to master Time watch how it masters you,
Learn Well,
let it teach you to master itself.
Then you will enter timelessness
and there you will find
effort
is not the Key
but knowing when to act incisively without seeping energy.
Learn to become sensitive to energy loss.
Learn its effects.

Life is the Treasure
Love is the Carrier
Morning comes
See Her Star

Thought 8
On power

Be careful what You give Power To,
give anything Power and It Will Wield It.
You can't then complain,
you gave it the power.
Think of Fear
give it power and you will experience
Fear.
Fear can't hurt you
but it will
if
you give it power to.

Life is the Treasure
Love is the Carrier
Morning comes
See Her Star

Thought 9
On Estrangement.

Estrangement and Exile
are
worse than death.
Beware.
Neither do it to yourself
or
another.

Life is the Treasure
Love is the Carrier
Morning comes
See Her Star

Thought 10
On Love

Love can really Hurt.
Balance

Life is the Treasure
Love is the Carrier
Morning comes
See Her Star

On Separation

The Dark night of the Soul
(John of The Cross and Song of Songs)

The lover calls out in the darkness,
No reply from the Beloved.
Alone, the Heart open,
weeping.
                         A hand not seen
                               stretches out.
But the Lover cannot see it.

The wasting comes with tears,
a hand reaching out,
but none
to touch.
                         Unseen a caress,
                           a tear removed
The Lover does not see.

The eyes dry,
the sting remains,
lost with no tears
left to fall.
                         Eyes water full,
                             watch.
The Lover does not see.

No sleep,
but it comes.
Despair at the traitorous
flesh.
                         A hand, tear stained,
                            reaches out.
The Lover does not see.
Shadows move,
     rainbows crumble.
         The Lover does not See.

                       Hands, eyes, lips meet,
                           once more.
                         The Lover sees.

Flow

My Love,
shadows we are,
drifting,
unseen,
un moving.
Here,
touch My Heart.
The Lover sees.

Walk, float, move We can.
None will Understand,
but,
Those who Lovers and Beloveds are
and feel
the open Heart.
This open Heart weeps in separation.
This open Heart it weeps in reunion.
This Heart lies open weeping,
binding joy to sorrow,
sorrow to joy
Now the Lover sees,
Ecstasy.
And what do the Lovers do?
What is Their solemn Vow?
To Care
and Love,
but most of all,
to safeguard the Open Heart.

On the Body

Watch your body well.
Sense
its imbalances.
Sense
when tiredness comes creeping
and disturbs
your balanced emotions,
turns them into fires,
floods,
empty rivers.

Guard your energy,
draw on the sources which
succour you.

Learn to sleep well

Train yourself to see
and study
your aura,
sense its working and responses,
sense its delicate weaving.

Eat well
and
gratefully
whenever you can.

Health is not a given.

On Suffering

Trust and Knowledge,
not belief which suffers doubt with its ebbs and flows,
are the Keys.

Jesus didn't know
He would survive beyond the cross.
He knew
His Father and His Father's Word
so He accepted the cross and the pain
This is deeper,
sacrifice.

Buddha
did not know He wouldn't starve to death.
But He Knew
That which He Sought
so accepted the pain.

This is deeper,
sacrifice.

Odin
hung on the Tree of Life.
He did not Know he would live on.
He knew That which He trusted.
He accepted the pain.

This is deeper,
sacrifice
Ghandi
took the Rifle Butt
not knowing if India would be free.
He took the bullet,
forgave His assassin
knowing That in which He trusted.

This is deeper,
sacrifice.

On my Being a Human
The uncertainty of what being Human means.

I can't wear platitudes.
I'm human,
with a condition.

This Love hurts,
exposes,
heals!
How does that work?
Why is acceptance so difficult?
Who is?
Am I?
What is to reject,
Why would you reject?

I cannot hide behind platitudes
I'm Human
and
Loving It!!

On Light and Dark

When dark is as light,
light is as dark,
the time for the lonely
has finally come.
Alone or together
is a choice you will make.
Prophecy without specificity is a wild rambling.
Is darkness light without light?
Is light darkness without darkness?
So is Nothing Everything without Everything?
So is Everything Nothing without Nothing?
So What do you see,
what Do you see,
what do You see,
what do you See?
What Do you see,
what Do You see,
what do You See?......
Depends on the question.

Against.
Now I stand,
old,
ancient,
outside your sacred archives,
what mean they?
Suddenly as the Light crushes and crashes
all,
I see,
shadows

See our special days,
festivals,
beware
all days are Holy.
Celebrate the Wheels of course,
but be aware of the dangers,
who can judge if one day is more special than another
or better than the one before?
None.

<u>On Doubt</u>
(James's letter)
So
the mirror of Doubt,
sworn enemy of belief,
you challenge?
Not weary of its tossing, ebbing, flowing, mercilessness?
You challenge.
I enter freely
arms open.
No Doubt,
The Mirror Smashes.
No Mirror therefore No doubt

So
the mirror of Belief,
sworn enemy of Doubt,
you challenge?
Not weary of its tossing, ebbing, flowing, mercilessness?
You challenge.
I enter freely
arms open.
No Belief,
The Mirror Smashes.
No Mirror therefore No Belief.

Time now to enter in
no doubt,
no belief,
only Knowing.

Flow

Thoughts on internal strife and when to ground yourself.

When 1

When mind wrestles with fear,
doubt with clarity,
confusion with certainty,
heart with spirit,
or mind,
or body,
or some with all.

When 2

Colder,
Hotter,
Changing.
Prepare for which?
The fibres are silent.
The vision unclear.

When 3

Panic is the demon
which drives out all within us that would cry,
THINK!
THINK!
THINK!

Flow

When 4
(In agreement with F. Herbert)

Fear truly can kill the mind.
A necessary part
of our
Psyche
put there for our protection.
It can remove knowledge leaving the mind
ineffective.
Hold lightly against fear.
Blocking,
or fighting,
gives it power.
Let it be as a wind,
a storm which requires weathering.

When 5

To be sure of
a sign
leads to finite choices.
So
what if the
sign
is wrong?
What then?

When 6

Watch,
listen,
weigh carefully.
Hold onto a vision tightly
but be prepared let it go,
as if molten metal was in your hand.
The crippled hand ceases
to be
as useful as it was.

When 7

Be as one with
the wind.
Probing, searching, stormy, gentle,
but always travelling, watching, listening,
throughout the kingdoms.

When 8

Guard all things well.

In The Void

Floating,
in the nothingness,
darkness,
I was.
Floating,
timeless,
spaceless.

Paths lit up the dark,
Golden,
Bright,
Flowing,
Powerful,
Independent,
each beautiful in its own right.
Sometimes weaving but never melding.
Flowing onwards.
never up
nor down
or
left
or right
but onwards through the void
where time has no meaning and space and direction
have no meaning.

Gliding,
swooping closer,
I saw where the paths slowed,
choked, then
burst onwards.
What is this?
Closer
Closer
Huge edifices,
like plaque on ivory teeth,
crumbling,
stilted the flow briefly.

Flow

A Voice.
'These are the temples of men.
The lobster pots,
the butterfly nets,
the bird cages of vibrancy.
Where enlightenment became entrapment,
a desire for upward not onward.
Structure over form.
Position over understanding.
Giving directions where none existed.
Each enlightened by analogies of their own time and not the path.
Light choked.'

'These are where town and city leader mentalities
put their human hierarchical controls
alongside
constraints of access
to and on
the paths.
Intentions mixed,
Some high,
some low.
Restricting the path,
requiring violent shaking to free itself
and then flow on unstoppable..
through their ruins.

In Darkness
(On Paul's question)

Faith
Love
or Hope?
When is each more stronger than the others?
Are not faith and hope not similar and dissimilar?
Interesting.
Faith in....
trust and expectation based on knowledge of experience
can be shattered by let down.
Love can be lost.
People seem to recover
mostly
from both but with
less
trust.
Most do not recover from lost hope,
Hope..
expectation based on desire.
It is hope that the
starving,
lost,
stranded
all cling to.
If Hope goes
they do too,
they give up.

On Being Equal

All here are equal.
In success and failure
Equal
In usefulness
and uselessness
Equal
In knowledge
and lack of it

Equal
Look neither up
nor down but
at others.

In Equality all are
empowered
to serve and humbly instruct.
To bow in respect is not
to be
subservient in
fear.

Here we serve
and are served by
all kingdoms
and existences
within the cosmos
including the
unseen realms
around
above
within
and below.

The Will in Service

Many times we put our feet through
A tapestry of experience.
This is our will walking
to learn flexibility.

Our feet will walk over broken glass.
This is our will
Being taught empathy
with the
crushed
and
broken
Who still sparkle in sun and moonlight
as diamonds.

Our feet will walk through fire.
This is our will being
purged,
cleansed,
transformed.
These are the paths of the servant.
So be it.

Sometimes our feet walk through soft, warm earth.
They will warm with
comfort and light.
This is the way of the servant.
So be it.

Many times we will walk through water.
This is our will being
cleansed,
and refreshed
This is the way of service
so be it.

Flow

Many times our feet will walk in and on air.
Our will is being revitalised,
uplifted,
energised and cleansed.

These are the paths of the servant.
So be it.
Focus then on what is to be done
and
do it.

Why?

Many ask
Why am I here?
Who am I?
What am I?
Why am I?
Maybe if we think,
I Am,
we'll
get all the
answers
we need.

Small Learnings Post 2011

(In answer to an overheard question arising after a group mediation to a situation which was,
"So what's in all this for me?")

What's in it for the Servant?

A voice asked
So what's in this for the servant?
So
I asked the same question.
This service,
this place of servant hood,
what's in it for the servant?
Silence.
Then

My teacher came. "Come walk with me through time and place. Then tell me what you have learnt."

So we walked…along a filthy street of poisoned water and air. Flats looming like ghostly shadows. The sounds of arguing, fights, babies crying, the plastic tunes of adverts, chat shows, canned laughter filled the air. Girls dressed in little, huddling in dim doorways taunting men.

A window opens above us, a woman gasps, runs inside, down stairs, out into the street to us. "My baby…please.." My Teacher instructs me to wait. It felt like an age passed.

The sounds and smells allured and repelled my senses. Soon my Teacher returned.

"Will it live?"
"Why does it matter?"
"You know though….don't you?"

"If I wanted to."
"What did you tell her?"
"That's between us, but tell me, what are you thinking?"

The teacher turned to me as the question hovered between us. We stopped. My teacher looked at me and continued. "All life is precious, better to live, hmmmm? Look around you – think."

Then I reflected on the squalor and hopelessness. I thought, 'there's always hope but....'
"What would you have done?" My teacher's voice cut in on my churning.
"..and said to her, especially when she looks you in the eyes and asks you, "Will she live?""
"I..I would have done what I could, then looked at the joy of making it....but the life, the love.......and then"
"Yes?"
"....that parting brings both sorrow and eternal presence, but both paths into life or death are hard for the living."
"So, what's in it for you? Let's walk on."
An arm strengthened my shoulders and we moved on.

We crossed a busy road, dodging angry drivers struggling to see through overloaded wipers. As we rounded a corner there were two men arguing and pushing each other. Two women hugged each other in a doorway sobbing.
Children, scared, wide eyed, shivering, clutched frantically at their dresses. Seeing the teacher, the two men paused but then continued. My teacher walked towards and between them, thrusting them apart.

I could not hear what was being said. Eyes alternated between anger, shame, stubbornness and compliance. The two women signalled their children to wait and each took hold of a man. they went through the doorway, silence, then the gentle rise of laughter.

"Well?" The teacher turned to me.
"I don't know."

"They were sisters, family meal, drinking. A misunderstood word, response anger, a fight, fuelled by their view of history long forgotten. So what would you have done and said?"
"To look at their wives and think of their children. That tomorrow they'd regret doing something over a foolish word, fuelled by inaccurate perspectives of events long ago and drink."
So what's in it for you? Let's walk."

We wandered through dimly lit streets, angry shop fronts, boarded, turned a corner into what felt like a war zone. Gun shots, screams, fighting and then we saw him. A young man slumped on the kerb. His blood mingling with the rain, I thought of a mother's tears. The teacher walked over, raised him a little, spoke a little. Their eyes met. Gently the teacher closed the young man's eyes and laid him down as you would a baby. I was shaking. "A gang war, territory incursions, drugs and girl profits. He was sixteen." Eyes bored the usual question into me.
"I....I don't know. Maybe that he was leaving all this pain, it would soon be over and there some who loved him, always would, and that I would be with him in his crossing over?"
"So, what's in it for you?"

"Yes but this is easy. Streets of squalor, poverty, this is not my world!?"

Everything changed. Sleepy middle class suburbia. Trees lined wide, clean pavements.
"Listen. What do you hear?"

"Weeping, fighting, arguing, but behind walls and closed doors and windows. I hear a woman sobbing, lonely, alone, imprisoned by her boundaries, brothers arguing over long distances reduced by the telephone but fuelled by perceptions of events and drink."
"What would you tell them, each has their own suffering and joys. Would you define suffering by degrees? How can you judge by degrees? Suffering is suffering to the sufferer."
"I..that....hmmm, I see the walls and distance are both as an illusion so stay closer to your family, friends and children. At least the sisters in the ghetto had each other."
The teacher indicated to move on added, "So. What would be in that for you?"

We walked and slipped through time and space, each the same as I saw before. Even from above, our planet was simply an extension, by degrees, of the ghetto and suburbia. Nation on nation, tribe on tribe, family on family. People, small problems crippling them, then others with huge problems crippling them. Others with similar difficulties dealing and blooming with them. All different and changing places depending on what they faced.

We stopped.
" So what's the answer to your question, for I have none." The teacher looked at me.
"Nor do I."
"Welcome to the great mystery. What makes a person willing to serve tick and also requires no answer to the question? Meditate on this briefly, then move on. There's work to do."

I meditated, then saw how, due to familiarity and over use, certain platitudes were, for those who require no answer to the question, not on little mounted pictures in the home but consciously expressed in their actions and life.

Lending
that requires no repayment
but expresses gratitude when it occurs

Loving
that requires no response
but expresses joy when it happens.

Touching
that requires no response
but expressed warmth if it happens.

Respecting
which requires no response
but expresses openness if it happens.

A knowing when help and support must be withdrawn
with no guilt
just understanding.

Avoiding of becoming a crutch
which inhibits development
and growth in others.

Flow

Knowing when it is time to let go, move on
without waiting for recognition.

Accepting mistakes are made
but learning from each one
and moving on.

Acceptance of the
unseen life
that occurs in the
shadows of people's lives,
soon forgotten.

Accepting transience
in all situations.
Learning how to give,
share,
receive,
freely.
Most of all,
eyes firmly seeing things

through the path
of Light,
supported by those
who passed this way
before .

Knowing when I am
out of my depth
and be able
to say so
without any concern or fear
over
losing face.
I cannot serve based on whether
it is or isn't

Flow

deserved
or
not wanted.

Sense a person's heart, not just their mind, words, deeds
and then
serve.
Remember Beauty and the Beast.

Reflect,
be self aware
or as is the 'in word'
mindful,
accepting,
honest of
and to
yourself.
These ensure the servant always starts from humility and understanding of
human fragility
which is in all.

This becomes
more
normal,
natural
as you
and
the Light become
closer
and in the end you are
less and less
seen
by
others.
So be it.
Time to move on.
There's work to be done.

On Psychic protection
be beyond your personal history
and
lost
in the light.

On rigidity of thought and action
(Inspired in part by F. Herbert)

1

Sometimes accusations and rumours come and ears burn.
If within them there is truth,
admit it humbly,
ask for forgiveness,
reconciliation,
reunion.
That is the only key.
The fear of gossip,
exile,
turned away eyes
can be avoided.
If repentance is rejected
then we must learn
to be as the grass
and lilies are
when the wind blows hard.
Fear prevents thinking.
The fear of losing
self respect
and respect from others,
especially
when not deserved,
can neutralise
clear
thinking.
Always attempt reconciliation three times,
maybe more when it is family.

2

Sometimes words and accusations
are false and unjust.
Again fears arise,
this is especially so
if

Flow

there is the added sting
of your explanations
are not believed in
and given credit
when they are the truth.
Here again
watch how the
grasses
and lilies
behave in the breeze.

3

To fail to learn
how to let
these fears
just pass
around
you
can lead to rigidity of thought,
the rabbit in the headlights,
and action
based
on old behaviour patterns.

They can lead
to a retaliatory
or pain dishing behavioural pattern.
Here observe how
rigid plants
are snapped

easily
by the wind.
In us
this means we hurt
only ourselves,
slide into self pity,
and sometimes

Flow

resentful
withdrawal.

4
Recognise
ancestral
behaviour patterns
received through our parents,
early lives,
grandparents,
beyond
and other family histories
shared over time
including our wider family.
Recognise those learnt
from siblings,
friends
or others.
Recognise
your father's
behaviour
in yourself.

The sayings,
'chip off the old block,
just like her mother,
his brother use to be like that',
serve
as
indicators.
Recognise
repetitive
behaviour patterns
in ourselves
which give
a temporary
personal sense of
self satisfaction,

Flow

self justice,
but hurt others.
In the end
they lead
to a numbing
of conscience
or worse
a weighty,
immovable
sense of guilt,
self estrangement
or self exile
as yet again
we hurt ourselves
because
we have no strategies
for fear.
Avoid a
'cut off your nose to spite your face'
strategy.

Recognise
patterns
which lead us into
a wilderness
of loneliness
on principal.

Recognise
those actions which we
would
rather
others
hadn't seen
or known about.

All these behaviours
begin
with a 'response thought'
leading to a decision.
Fear
can
prevent
use of thought
from occurring
in this crucial gap
between
event
and reaction
or response to the event

It is the development of the
awareness of this
gap
between
event
and response
which
begins
flexibility
and reduction of fear and fears.

5

In a storm
some plants
break,
lose the odd limb
or flap about
but survive
with only the loss of
a flower head or two.

Flow

Degrees of
flexibility
or rigidity is
the issue for us too.

It is normal to
experience
highs and lows,
sometimes we get an excess of one or the other.
Anger is a useful emotion.

It isn't wrong to have anger
but it is down to us
what we do with it
which leads to a
snap
or
development
and growth.

Self awareness
and reflective abilities
need to be developed
and put to use in the
event-response gap.
Personality is
distinct
from developing self awareness
in this way.
Quiet peaceful and calm people
often keep things
in and end up with
stomach issues
while the fiery,
maybe,
get more
blood pressure.

6

An event
triggers memories and old patterns
this can be the beginning of fear
fear of repetition of responses which hurt
fear of repeating failure
This is also the gap
where thought is possible
before a response
is given.

This is the gap where
we will
be flexible
or
rigid
Ask yourself
Where is my considered response coming from?
What or whose behaviour is
this
that I am
considering?
What might be
the outcome of a response to
myself
or others?

If negative response is to be given,
is the self justification
to be at the cost
of
social and emotional exile or estrangement
worth it?

What has the real effect
of a similar planned behaviour used in the past
achieved for myself

Flow

or others?
Was there
a winner
or loser
when the concept of
winning or losing
wasn't appropriate
previously
to the event
but only to
the patterned behaviour.

Invariably we are
the loser
when fear
is
given
the power
to
prevent
clear thought
in the gap
between
triggering event

response.

7
Once the process of
spotting this gap begins
perseverance is required.
Doubts,
emotions will flood in the early work.
Especially
when the
outcome doesn't seem
as positive as we hoped.
Over time

Flow

we will begin
to see ourselves
more accurately
and adapt
our behaviour
accordingly
to reducing the
hold of fear
which facilitates
seeing and experiencing
more
light
which
strengthens
us.

Flow

I don't believe in anything – why bother to light a candle?

We all use
candles
for
different purposes.
However,
most
of these are about creating
a certain ambience
or
mood.

People light candles
when in the bath,
listening to music,
for special dinners,
courtship.
We now extend this
to when we're having
a barbecue
or camping.
More people want some form of
real fire
in their homes.
The question
is
why?

Some of us remember
that going to Nan's
was always special
because of
the real fire,
special candles at Christmas
or the wonderful
bonfires
of
November 5th.

Candles seem to
help our moods.
They enhance

Flow

that special courtship period,
the dinner party
with
friends.

Candles give light,
some heat
and
so much more.
Another use is
to help maintain
a thought for ourselves
or another
while we get distracted.
Non-religious people
have done this
for centuries.

Go to the place
where Marc Bolan
or some other celebrity died.
There are often
candles burning
which represent
continuing thought
and
regard.

We often light a candle
for others here
for exactly this purpose,
to maintain and represent
our love and concern for them
at a distance.
We can't think of someone continually
but the candle
represents our wish
that we could.

So…why not light one for yourself or another..if not here then at home.
Thinking of you…

Sometimes we feel better by simply
opening the curtains or

Flow

turning on the
light.

Next time you blow out a candle
reflect on how words
carried on
your
breath
can snuff out
love,
joy,
friendship,
self esteem
and even
hope.

Flow

<u>The Streams of Blood and Tears 1</u>

And what will be the crown of
of our Tri-Partite
expression?
Choice.
I see disharmony
Then let there be harmony
I Am a stream of blood,
from us,
the source.
I Am a stream of tears,
from us,
the source.
Blood and tears
Red and white
from a single
source.
What then expression?

Sensitive to Our Blood,
a Spirit.
Sensitive to Our Tears,
a Soul.
And what of the expression?
Psyche,
Emotions,
a body,
in one
inseparable.

Let there be Light.

The Streams of Blood and Tears 2

These Streams
flowing out
from one source
where do they go?

Neither their beginning
nor
end
is perceivable.

As one lies in a bed
another hangs on a tree
wounded,
two streams,
one source
where do they go?
two streams
where
do they go?

Streams of Blood and Tears 3
(After trying to grasp the Western Tree of Life)

I arose,
befuddled and understanding
nothing.

Columns,
spheres,
spheres within spheres,
whirled.
Something called out
but was
lost in the chaotic consciousness
of dreaded trigonometry
of lines
and
spheres.

Fears,
memories,
flooded back.
Maths,
the squared blackboard,
the accurately thrown chalk
meeting my forehead,
just for whispering,
I don't get this...
am
I
stupid?

Flow

The
Tree,
Sacred
Tree,
Place of Sacrifice and Redemption..
long
before
Jesus.
Spear,
Heart,
Two
rivers,
One
Source.

The wounded King,
The two maidens,
Leaves of Light.
Two streams
one source

As I rose
rubbing forehead,
remembering the chalk
I saw them.

The tree of diagram
rose
to obscure out
my chaos.

Blood flowing
down the left
Tears flowing
down the right
none had said a word about this,
nothing had I read,
about this.
Suddenly
memories flooded in
and
I
understood.

Flow

Streams of Blood and Tears 4

On the doubtful
wisdom
and use
of the phrase
'Blood is thicker
than
water'

Scientifically
liquids
aren't compared
by
thickness
but
chemical complexities in their make up.

Blood is thicker than water..
the cause of unnecessary
revenge,
pain
and
not measured thought
maybe.
An excuse for the perpetual bullying
of
another
family.
Innocence and guilt,
irrelevant.

Blood is thicker than water...
means care,
standing up for,
looking out for
those
of your blood.Truth,
irrelevant.

Cosmically
they are equal,
and simply represent
necessity

Flow

due
to
manifestation and expression
and
the gift
of
choice
which gave birth
to
the
redeemer
before
creation and expression
even
began.

A more useful reflection
I think.
Choose well.

Late 2015
Gist 1

On Stillness and not fearing a place of Dis-Ease
(A Play of 1 scene in response to Jacob Boehme's
The Signature of All Things and the works of RJ Stewart & Anastacia Nutt.)

A single actor stands with back to audience looking into a projection of the night sky. One actor but with different colour lights defining the Mind(Psyche)/Green, Soul / Red/& Spirit/White as required.

Narrator: Psyche looks into the darkness through the eyes.
Psyche:
I must be unwell, in a state of dis-ease. The expression, the body which carries me, is fit enough.
There is money in the bank.
We have work...just enough and we eat well.
Why am I dis-eased? Nothing satisfies.
None of my friends, even the closest, get this. They laugh, with rather than at me, but see no reason for dis-ease.
'Too serious', they say, heartily patting me on a confused wincing shoulder, whilst ordering another pint.
Feelings, why do you sleep? Why isn't anger, despair, sadness or anything stirring in me? This dis-ease feels flat and ominous.
The darkening clouds, hints of the Thor, stoking a bellow enraged furnace, raising the Hammer. Destructive Zeus weighing, checking His javelins of silver streaks of pain, Creation and refreshment with crows circling wildly and loudly.
Flat. Nothing. No Star to guide, no words come from anywhere except platitudes of meaningless adverts deemed worthy of the title, Spiritual Platitudes of Truth which say nothing of this nothingness.
Sleep comes....so slowly...but it comes.

Narrator: Soul Addresses Spirit
Soul Addressing Spirit:
At last I'm asleep. Come Spirit, now there is stillness in the expression, what happens now? How is this mind to find us, our meaning and therefore its' own context and meaning?
Odd, only in sleep are we released to wander to where once we came from
full of expectations of Divine Union
and not
dreams,
as what our expectations have become,

of re-Union with
the Breath
who spoke into nothing...
"Let there be Light".

Spirit:
This mind, in this expression, sees much, senses much, but is clouded by choice, life and fears. Where there is no fear there flows in flawed logic with formulae such as 1 + 2 = 4 because of a dislike of seemingly untidy odd numbers.
The knowledge of the relationship that
Religion + History = Bloody Wars and senseless killing, torture and pain, therefore no God, a classic 1+2=4.
But the Dis-Ease stems from knowing this is flawed logic but knowing nothing to challenge it.
Also, and for us, the most difficult,
Vivid Dream of floating through Cosmos + any spiritual encounter = possible madness or silence for fear of that accusation or a personal judgement that too much fantasy has been watched and should be avoided for a while.

Soul:
But we are two thirds of our expression. How odd that, whilst we, the carriers of the Divine Spark or Signature of All Things, are a majority in this expression or body, it has the 'Joker', or the 'trump'. Choice. But we three are one yet we are, well, seemingly at odds?

Spirit:
Yes.
This is the nature of the logic and the resultant answer is
a wilderness flat of emotion and Dis-ease. Here nothing satisfies, tastes or feels right. Nothing seems beautiful or inspiring awe. The world is grey as are all those who walk in it. There is no longer surprise at atrocity or horrific events, they are expected. There is an empathic human response of money but a hollowness as there is no identification due to Our disconnection from One another. You and I dance between our divine aspect, past experiences whilst our expressed nature sleeps, ignorant with Dis-ease and yet knowing...hence...Dis-ease
(Backdrop of night sky fades into darkness/no light on actor)

Psyche:
I know this place, here there is nothing. Yet there is everything. My conception and destruction yet Peace. Space for Soul, Spirit and Mind to see through one pair eyes, sense through One Heart and Understand in One Mind. Joy of Expression.

Spirit, Soul & Psyche (Actor lit by the three colours)
Eyes opened and closed in nothing. Seeing everything and nothing. Peace. Stillness.
(The backdrop now lights –up and fades non-rhythmically)

Actor:
This is my beginning and my end. The centre, the Creator. Here everything is flowing from and to.
Here there is everything and nothing.
My Dis-ease has led to non-resistance to nothing, stillness.
Mind, Soul and Spirit flowing as one so the body, the outer expression, may become and reflect, through choice, the joy of being Expression of the One behind everything.
Stillness.

Flow

Gist 2
(On Paracelsus and Simonedes with thanks to RJ Stewart who introduced their works to me.)

The Bubble Pot
&
The Tears

'Grandad'

'Yes'

'Can you tell me another adventure of what you've seen?'

'That depends on whether you can use your imagination'.

'I think ….I think I can.'

'Good, get your little bubble pot and blow a bubble. Good…look at the largest one…what do you see?'

'I see swirling colours on the skin, and little bubbles in bubbles. I've never looked for long before…it was about blowing the biggest bubble and bursting it!'

'What could there be in your little bubble world?'

'Wow..Harry Potter?..oh no you've told me before to come up with my own pictures…castles, knights, dragons, faeries, people all mixed up and living together…and planets and people travelling without space suits?'

'Well done..now burst your bubbles but remember them or this adventure will drift over you and be lost like your bubbles.'

I was in France…I was younger..and it was wonderfully hot. I actually was using the air conditioning in the car I had hired. I was heading for the ferry and had stopped at a strange place where life size statues depict the lead up to and death of someone called Jesus.'

'I've heard of Him I think..at school'

'Good, now alongside the wide empty roads of France, you'll often see what looks like a little house cut in half so you can see inside. And in this there is a statue of Jesus on the cross. Despite being by a road they are usually clean and surrounded by flowers and little cards with prayers on them.'

'Why?'

'Remember our visit to that little church in Wales?'

'Oh Yes, where the lady protected a Hare from the King..there was a little mini church and there were cards..is that it?'

'Yes, now the odd thing was… I decided to pull over for a break and a bit of bread and cheese. Opposite the little lay-by was one of these little houses but it was filthy. Now, don't ask me why, but I had plenty of water and a cloth so I decided to clean it. I wasn't and am not now a religious person as you know. It took quite a while until it gleamed like the others. I stopped and stood up and that is when this adventure began.'

'I was looking at the little statue and I saw I'd left a drop of water in the right eye, I bent to wipe it …it wasn't a drop..it was a tear!!'
'Wow..what did you do?'
'I thought it was the heat and my lack of glasses. I got my hat from the car, soaked it and put it on, that was bliss. I went back cooler and armed with glasses. I went back and it was still there…I puzzled. I thought then about why had it been so dirty?'

'Because Madame Flambert, who use to tend it, is with me now.' It was gentle voice, calm and yet..

I was scared now and thought of how long I'd stood in the heat. You are wise at this point to look at me quizzically grandson. I'd never heard voices before and all that that meant..heatstroke, madness, doctors..All rose up in me. But the voice broke in again.'
'You know there is more to the story than leaving Me on an image which was only half of the story.'

'Aaah, your disillusion?...Once you were like the future bride in Solomon's song. But then your enthusiasm coated you like too much oil...I knocked, but you couldn't open the door anymore and since then you've run wretched through life...finding pale substitutes until now. Throw the tear into the air in front of you.'
'Oddly I did just that…and..it grew into a large beach ball size sphere. I could see so many colours, blue, white, red, black, green and also metals, and something else. 'What's that?', pointing to the middle of the sphere I asked.'
'What can you see?'
'It's like ball of utter blackness…it makes me feel calm and terrified. …and there's something else but I can't understand or grasp it.'
'Well, you once searched through thousands of academic papers, held them

in memory, and looked for gaps in research I believe, but you can't grasp this…what is it you tell your grandchild to do when he asks you for one of your adventures…such as the Weave?'

'Use imagination…but then it's not …oh…The Web is real, as I showed him through sharing imagination…'
'And?'
'Gods and Goddesses I suppose…but that's odd I thought , according to…please I mean no disrespect…but I thought with Yourself..there was only One God?'
'Just carry on.'
'In the centre Sphere it seems empty and yet full..this I also feel ..well I feel winds, air…Life. …and…I don't get this.'
'Hmmmm?'
'Well I see Angels…in there', pointing to the spheres, 'the Angel is tiny but I sense it is beyond my biggest concept of enormous….bigger than a planet..possibly a galaxy. But then.. ….a Sword, a Chalice, Shield & Staff?' I was looking at this when I glanced down at the figure…another tear.

I stooped down, it felt a little colder, silvery. I sensed what to do and now I knew what my grandson went through when I advised him to use his imagination. Another sphere appeared but it appeared around and in the first sphere. I paused..not sure how or what to ask.'
'This sphere, what do you see?'
'I still see the still, dark centre but the second sphere is both within and without the first sphere as if they are three spheres and not, It has brought about a change, it's influencing the blue and green…well rivers…but now I see another thing which seems to be rather odd….I see a red stream …of blood.. coming from the same root or spring as a stream of…water..more like tears as well…I can't even grasp this using my imagination.'
'Look at my little house'.
'Oh , there are two streams flowing out of Your Image…but I feel that what I am seeing in the spheres…comes before You.'
'Correct & not'

'This second sphere is affecting everything I noticed…especially liquids…like the moon does to the Earth. There was a silence as this little thought went in. I reflected now on what I was looking at..The first tear became the Earth so this one..is the Moon.'

'Well grandson, this continued until there were seven spheres, each one affecting the others and they formed inwards and outwards. Lots of colours, feelings and a great deal more. The sixth Sphere was between graspable and not. It felt like the greatest Joy but at the greatest Price willingly paid. I wondered whether this was where the Voice was..but I didn't ask and wasn't told…There's a lesson there…remember it. '
'Was that it then granddad?'
'No.'

'Then it was odd. What's happened…what's that? I pointed to the ever moving spheres. Something has seemingly blurred out all spheres…both inside and out? As I said this…Another tear appeared…as I stooped I felt…wrong…I shouldn't touch this one….should I?'
'Why not?'The Voice cut in.

'It's what's happened to the Spheres…that….that layer..it feels deliberate… like a bottomless pit, and weirdly..It's like an uncrossable river and there are things on the far side of it..like…what you see in a famine but much worse. This new tear feels different.'
'You are right…it is…but it is only a tear …..so take it.'

'I did and weirdly it enveloped the strange area but also appeared inside all the other spheres…This was too hard to describe…then I noticed there were sort of bridges across the …hmmm… not nice layer…. This happened with the next tear as well. These two tears felt very different to all the others…as if all the first tears and spheres were actually made by or born from these last two spheres which, a bit confusingly, were also inside all the other spheres.
I thought it was all over, when a tear appeared but it …this is simply to help you understand it grandson…it was sort of black..it was almost as if it wasn't there, like it was nothing but as it grew it enfolded all the other spheres. It reminded me of the centre of the first sphere. I almost wanted to be inside it…oddly I wondered if it would be like being nothing. There was another thought or imagining…it was out of this last sphere that all the others came …and..well you'll have to wait a while for that part grandson.'

'So. What do you see and sense now?' The Voice returned.
'Strange things, images really. Pervading the first to seventh sphere I sense there are others, I don't know..'
'Mysteries?'
'YES…Mysteries.
I also sense images moving between and through the Spheres, like communications but not spoken, maybe they are sort of memory holders. I see a boy about to walk over a cliff and yet suddenly he looks like an Old Man with a lamp. I see a Star, Moon..I'll have to think about this…'

I waited for the voice but there was no voice, the images of the spheres began to move towards me. They completely enfolded me and then shrank inside me…as if they had always been there.

I became aware of a woman next to me. I smiled and said hello and forgot to speak French. She nodded and in a heavily accented voice introduced herself, Madame Flambert. She bent down to the little statue and carefully removed the nails, I expected her to pick the ivory like statuette up but it collapsed into her waiting hands…a tiny crucified human figure…then it seemed to …well sort of…develop backwards into baby form and then was gone.

There was a sigh from the little house. The cross's side arms had dropped to the centre to make an equal armed cross. I went to speak but she indicated silence…a rose grew from nowhere in the centre of the four arms and a red tear formed on the left spar and a white tear on right spar.
She bent down and lifted this cross, placed it into my hands, signalled to hold it to my chest when suddenly she and it disappeared. I remained silent for some time and then saw how the little house had an outline of the old cross. I cleaned it up just as the French police pulled up.

They thought I had stolen the crucifix. After searching myself and the car they accepted my story….you know..a mad idea, but clean the empty house ….and that was it. That is the adventure of The Tears.'
'Wow..so..?'
'You know the rule, three questions and then that's it.'
'Ok…I assume that like sensing the Weave in the Web of life, when I get a little older, if I can learn to be…still..I might see these for myself?'

'Yes.'

'What does it all mean?...Oh I just wasted a question didn't I?...ok last question. How do you remember all of this?'
'What do I do when I have to go shopping which I hate and my memory is getting weaker?'
'You make a list and put it on the kitchen table. You then imagine the kitchen with the table and list'
'Why?'

'Because it is naughty to leave things on the table Nan says. Then you picture a cartoon duck dancing on the imagined table...because you hate cartoon duck and it's wrong to dance on the table. So you have to get him off it. You then picture the journey round the shops in the same way. When it's time to go shopping you go through your imagination, knock the cartoon duck off the table and pick up your list....oh..I already knew that..I wasted a question.'
'No, you asked three questions and then you have realised you already have some answers which you forget. So what did I store this adventure in?'
'My Bubble Pot!!!'
'Well in a way yes but it was the one I had as a child and that is where my memories of the Spheres are stored.
'Wow...next time I look into a bubble... ...I'm going to see much more...in fact...see you granddad..I'm going into the garden.'

Gist 3
All Hallows Eve

The Veil is thin now
October
the time of memory ,time of remembering
time of connection
blood time.

The veil is thin now,
connections,
the blood remembers
and
autumn stirs it into a drowsy waking.

The veil is thin now,
memories,
memories not lived through
and yet lived through
flood the blood
and touch
consciousness.

The veil is thin now,
partings and returnings,
dance in the blood,
stirring ancient memories,
of lives not lived
and yet lived.
The veil is parted,
for a brief time,
reconciliation.
October

Prelude

This sleeper, who in tales does sleep, a kiss,
say you, to stir and wake. Sleeps who or where?
What sleeps in all a kiss could stir or miss
this chance to wake for what or who? Is there
chance last if missed by I none kissed? How fare
this sleeper then? In cot in purple stone
lay I. Slept she on stone near me. Aware,
not she, of me but I of her alone.
Was I asleep in her or her in me? Not known.

White snow, thorn red, a spindle sharp to sleep
these ones did send. What dreams, what point to these
which come in dreams in mist when hazed then steep
these dreams in life do we commit and freeze
to live, as meaning lost like kites in trees?
Know I through sleeper's eyes the sleeper lies
in all alive to kiss awake. Who sees,
or knows, how kiss to self is done or tries
to show, to I, to wake the I asleep in lies?

In Malkuth's heart, unseen, there lies the all
the ev'rything, its end, its past, yet now.
In Malkuth's heart, unseen, is naught. To call
the all, yet naught, is fruitless task. But bow,
the mind, in stillness's void dark, like prow
of ship in eye of storm, where space and clock
do cease. No light no night to stir the vow
awake. Still be. This crown in sacred rock
asleep, awake for kiss. This All and Naught unlock.

In darkness, I a candle lit and stood
in stillness I became as naught, yet all.
Mind mine, with chat did seek distract, if could
remind of jobs done not or who might call
on phone, at door. Still be mind mine is all
ask I, command, demand of you this day.
Not me fail let so early on or fall
at this fence first upon this narrow way.
To stillness I returned at last could start to pray.

Oh East, of life the breath , birth new and spring.
Bright shines new equinox dawn sun. The Sword
of truth here mind does cleave. Here Druids sing
of sacred hills, the cleansing wind. The cord
of winter slain by staff of Oaken Lord.
Here feather, sword equal in power be.
Eagle, and Wren arrows first flew then soared.
Inspired am I in East and Air and see
so clear from Sacred heights. Now buds turn green the
tree.

In East is mighty Raphael. Here Life
begins, is held, is gifted to. Life's air
for being freely given out. Dawn's fife,
by wind and breeze now played, weaves tunes so fair
and light. Creep these , then seep in sleeper's lair
where creatures wake, then scratch, then yawn and stir.
Now winter's clasp lies broken, smashed. White hare
now dances, boxes, courts with gleaming fur.
Life's breath is East's fair gift so with your words don't
slur.

Flow

Oh South, the light and sun of solstice fire.
Fierce burns this noon day sun. Justice, with veil,
Rod hers, from South, now wields and does not tire.
Old bards now chant a life transforming tale
of Dragon's fire, a knights first time in mail
of lead. then golden light. A spear is thrust
at changeling foe. Through fur, feather and scale
it tests resolve's intent. From ash and dust
of southern fire the phoenix knight now he stand must.

In south does mighty Michael stand. Here light
begins, is held, is gifted to. Long days
for greening crop, mature youths work and fight.
Sigh alchemists as missed the path, a maze
made they of simple truth, sun's mighty rays.
This son bursts forth, comes light with life and peace.
Now child and seed of spring have left the haze
of mists which diamond flecked young lambs' white fleece.
Light's fire is South's fair gift. Transform. Light yours release.

Oh West, the water, rain, compassion's tears.
Now equinox of summer's leaving time
rings change. Here cauldron, grail flow out, ease fears
in Mabons laid on river green. No crime
was done and fate would help this bard to climb
to lofty heights. Now salmon seeks a sea
of wisdom deep. Old dancers weave and mime
the fall of golden leaves on bended knee
as soon the veil will part. From death can one not flee.

Flow

In West is mighty Gabriel. Here Love
begins, is held, is gifted to. Love flows
in tears, in blood. Now red sunset's above
are still as evening comes and daylight goes.
A wounded king gives blood, water who chose
path his with love. Now give and take or choose
as wise grandmothers do and be as rose
of love, an oak of strength. Love life pursues,
fears not a rising sun at night. This love won't lose.

Oh North, sacred is soil of earth and stone.
Low solstice sun dim rayed, too briefly bright
on hidden bear and Arthur's long cold throne.
Here Gwyn Ap Nudd a mighty shield upright
stands guard against the ruthless northern night.
Now raven wing beats slow in ruthless sleet
filled winds. These storms of death can nothing fight.
Crops our's to seed and land to sleep, too fleet,
too cold are days for work. In death again will meet.

In North is mighty Uriel. Here Law
begins, is held, is gifted to. Law stands
moved not by life or death. Dreamed I and saw
in darkened cave a Goddess spun with hands
wove my short lives from ends to ends. No bands
of bandits lurk in here. All rests a while
till Bridget stirs, with seeds walks she these lands.
In day's rhythms, a year, a life. A dial
for sun cast shadows track to death from babes' first
smile.

Flow

In centre I, in light of earth, was cloaked.
For I light born, light healed, light changed, light made.
A change in air, it stirs, a tap, who croaked?
A wing, on door, eyes turn, legs move. Afraid?
No no. In light strode I no fear delayed
a hand on door, a foot to step outside.
No hall, no rug, no lights nor music played.
Green hill, blue sky, no sun, yet bright, crows cried,
flew they with looks confused, a door and me who sighed.

Lush green soft grass greets foot. In scent filled air,
bees hum whilst clover kiss. Strange flowers sway
in gentle breeze. A downward trail, with care
moved I to brow of gentle slopes. The way
clear was. On far off hills and mountains play
a rainbow haze of misty hues. This trail
oft will this way both right and left now stray
to ancient grove so rich in greens not pale.
Like Arthur's quest, this distant grove to me is grail.

On narrow path sensed I those gone before
whose footsteps silent are, yet not. A change
in air, as grove now loomed. Saw I cranes soar
and patterns make which some well know. So strange
clues these but lost on me, beyond sight's range
soon glide. At portal's edge of grove must wait
head bowed then raised. Path I for grove exchange.
In centre ashes mark fires past a grate
of stone long cold. Sat I and poked, did guide await

.

Flow

At south west gate hare white appeared, and stares
a while, bowed I at nod, then rose to stand.
As through stepped I, in distant vale white mares
the way did show to ancient forest land.
White hare, takes leave a parting glance, then hand
raised I in grateful thanks. Through verdant green
passed I, then stopped, as grass did bend breeze fanned
showed stones, and feathers strange all tokens seen
oft times. To one drawn eye but wait. Comes She, serene.

A gentle doe, bowed I. 'One you may take'
as she at token looks and purse, then shows,
of velvet green. 'That shell from Arthur's lake,
of secret sword, once fed by sacred flows,
came long ago.' Turned I, gone she, just crows
now watch as stoop, place shell in purse and see
a symbol gold on velvet move. Still blows
the breeze as I am drawn to lone oak tree
who stands on edge of forest old and watches me.

Did stand by path through oak and ash with yew,
old birch and thorn and more obscured from sight.
As token seen, down path went I in view
of crows watched they from branches high as light
grew dim on forest path, no fear that might
stray lost. In foaming stream as minnows dart,
old salmon stay so still. Strange birds alight
on branches high. Wait they. What soon will start?
A bridge cross I , just trunk and rope. Slow down, poor heart.

Flow

Through gaps in trunks a bothy green is seen.
Now light seems brighter clearing's edge draws nigh.
Now breath is held at awesome sight as lean
on trunk old, gnarled but strong. 'It's huge' sigh I
as lover struck. Hand mine on heart, 'don't die.'
A grove, so vast. Green grass grazed short. No flock
in sight. Hill Small , in middle it does lie.
Now crowned by ancient stag. Whose eyes now lock
with mine. Bow I and sit by crystal ancient rock.

In air, now tense, change comes. Stag great then throat,
does stretch. Roars He a song so old and loud
which echoes round and round the grove. A moat
of song round mighty hill. Antlers so proud
then cease the song. Now silence falls, a shroud
laid soft. A man antlered , white stag, does greet.
In fur and green with mighty club 'twas vowed
what would be done then antlers shook. On seat
of stone to club sang he. Shapes strange did weave then meet.

Rose he, by stag, then stood. Club raised then laid
on hide of ancient fur. Once more a roar
the grove now filled. Both song and tune now played
had changed. Now harmonies not there before
from trees now filled the air, did weave and soar.
As steam did rise from ancient stag all ceased.
Both Lord and stag were still. Wait they. What for?
Then whispers, scuttles, flaps, around increased
as branches shook like ferns below came all released.

Flow

Here prey and hunter one, and still, in peace.
A change . On club strange shapes do weave on wood
and meet. Once more, on fur, club laid. All cease.
So insects, creatures, birds round hill all stood.
as gentle song then fills the air. None could
now move as song caressed and wooed, eased minds.
then voices joined once more and I now should
add mine. As I began knew I what binds
all things to all. Raised hand on hill as song unwinds.

Each one time found with antlered lord to talk.
Face his oft moved from sad to joy as news
told they. As bear and salmon speak, did walk,
and see both vole and fox give each their views.
Not mundane daily toil but close issues
fill their soft speech. As I with care do tread
a brown field mouse spot I near sacred yews.
Eyes mine it holds. On leaf of autumn red
the shell lay I then bowed. Its news now entered head.

A change . On club strange shapes do weave on wood
and meet. Once more, on fur, club laid. New song
as air still fell. Turned all. Oaks old now stood
by these stood she green clad. Black hair and long,
jet black eyes hers. Then oaks, so old, so strong
sang loud as Lord and Lady stand and gaze.
Bow they to stag and then to all the throng
in sacred grove where heart and voice did raise
in hymns and songs which life and season's ways did praise.

Flow

This time it seems is closing now as all
have turned to leave. All glance at sacred three
who bless and sing to parting friends then call
the ev'ning in. Heads three now turn to me.
Bow I then raise eyes mine. Turn they by tree
bow both to stag, as light begins to fade,
then leave. This stag now sings so wistfully
as forest he now leaves. Path mine in shade
of dimming wood slowly leave I as time now bade.

To grove then brow of hill climbed I then turned
and sat a while to muse on all that saw
and heard. Within head mine a message burned
from mouse to man came it. Stood I in awe
and bowed then turned to face the crow on door
where I had entered here. Croaked it, then flew
far far o'erhead alone was I once more.
Held I the door, felt oak, ash, thorn and yew
a fare well give. To stay or leave? But I this knew.

Through door passed I and sat in empty room.
The candle glowed a steady flame but bright.
Shadows ,strange shapes did weave which meet. A loom
it seems, on walls does weave dreams mine of light
and journeys far. Stand I. This flame keeps night
at bay. But now, bless I, as Ancients say,
this flame upon its way and thank for sight
this flame then snuff light out. Should I now pray?
No no. Through door, on rug, down stairs, Know I the way.

Flow

The Water of Life

(Brothers Grimm/ other tales Paul Hodgon)

In palace garden princes three did weep.
'Our father king is sick and death him trails.
To watch him die, no hope of cure. No sleep
would we now take. Of cure there are no tales.'
'A cure there is but each brave, bold, quest fails.'
Their gardener revealed.' Water of Life
its name. But danger lurks for he who sails.
Go east, take spear, a sword ,a bow and knife.
Go on your own. They say the way is laid with strife.'

So princes three their father begged to let
the eldest go. So ill got he, agree
did he. This son, armed he and blessed. So set
out fast this eldest son on land and sea.
This son was not as he did seem for see
in cold heart his lay greed. To cure the king
was his intent. The kingdom his set fee.
Brothers two hell could take as father's ring
was good as his. Rode he, then sailed, of greed did sing.

A dwarf, in road did block the onward way.
With horse, nudged he then swore and cursed then spat.
'Move old, worn dwarf, Water of Life which way?'
'If young master, more polite be, then that
now sought, may have, been shown.' Brushed he dropped
hat,
this wily dwarf, as down a road then stared.
'Hah fool! Gave you the road away! No chat.
For that road I will take.' horse whipped, not spared,
by master's greed. To road sped they. Love none here shared.

Flow

This road, steep sides, to close the way, began.
This son, ignored horse's unease. But there
was no retreat, no road behind. 'We can
go on,' Stopped he, looked back, no road from where
came he. Turned he to onward spur . Despair
felt he. 'That dwarf, plans mine, now dead.' Horse grazed
on grass, rich green, so close then reared, no care,
as rider fell, did him leave there. Amazed
it followed paths of green. Now son, alone, stood dazed.

Cursed he luck his, stones kicked, then swore, then spat. .
Watched he arms his, bread his with steed depart.
Oh whistle he in vain did try, then sat.
Steed his well knew what freedom meant. No heart
for whips or spurs nor kicks. So off did start
for home. But friendly dwarf some succour gave.
So home was found and work, a tiny cart.
Now angry prince for days and nights did rave.
No hope of hell for brothers two. Him they must save.

By king's sick bed now princes begged to send
the second prince for cure and first to seek.
This poor sick king, agree did he, to end
pleas theirs. Armed he then blessed this quest. But meek
or kind was not this second son. To speak
of greed, cold heart is closer truth. So start
did he, for cure and kingdom's gain. But cheek
with pride was flushed so red. But fate would part
this prince from horse in gorge. Steeds two, now pulled
dwarf's cart

Flow

So youngest son now sought this cure to end
poor father's pain. Soon he dwarf met. Dismount
did he and bread did share and cart did mend.
'Seek I a cure for father's ills, the fount
from which flows life. So friend must I remount.'
'This place know I,' this dwarf then spoke, ' and fate
now leads down yonder path. Take care to count
the hours that pass once through the castle gate.
These gates, at midnight close. King yours fail you if late.'

'Loaves two and iron wand give I to you.
Times three strike you on iron gate then throw
straight way, loaves these, to fierce lions two.
Wait they for those who enter there. Then go
and fill flask yours from fount. No slowness show,
don't wait but rush to leave. If midnight rings
then gates will close, quest yours is lost. Then know
from you blood yours and life shall flow as kings
of creatures feed. Flesh torn by birds, white beaked, black
wings.'

So prince, with loaves and wand, left dwarf and rode
to tower tall where castle door now shook
as wand times three did strike. Within there strode
two fearsome beasts but loaves tossed he. No look
got he. Eyes his did see thrones four in nook
where shadows danced. Then girl on him did fling
arms hers, then kiss . 'Now free, you my heart took
on entry here. Of you heart mine will sing,
come find home mine, now yours. Please take this golden
ring.'

Flow

'A kingdom ours will rule when next do meet
oh my love true .' Past gates ran she and light
in streamed on dusty thrones, and on each seat
a sleeping prince. Rings four them bound in night
like sleep. Each step, more light, no lamps in sight.
An open door revealed a bed. Sheets felt
so warm, a little rest sought he. On flight
of girl thought he . Came sleep to bind like belt.
In dreams did he a future seek in cards life dealt.

A bell. Leapt he. In pool flask his did place.
Then sped as gates did creak, then start to close.
Dived he through gap as gates did slam. Though race
was won heel his was torn. Sighed he, then rose
and limped to waiting, smiling dwarf who chose
gifts two from cart to give. 'This sword and bread
give I to you. Not mine to keep. One knows
not when these gifts to share . But keep cool head
as needs do rise. Do use them well or end up dead.'

'No war nor fight can sword e'er lose. So place
by shield on saddle worn. This loaf can feed
a thousand folk yet whole it stays. Now race
back home to cure your King so loved. So need
is met, quest yours is done. Now mount on steed,
with haste do fly. Not right, not left, do turn
but straight ahead to home, to cure, now speed.
Then seek for her who once heart your's made burn
and take hand hers . Of your own fate seeks she to learn.'

Flow

'Oh dwarf, thanks mine give I. But once had I
two brothers, who, also seek I to save.'
'Those men trapped I and there will stay, will die.
These black hearts hard, with joy, would you enslave.
To king, what you have won so hard when brave,
give life and claim this work as theirs. Then king
would rise, give all to sons, for you a grave
will dig. Then seek to steal bride yours and ring.
No bards of your great deeds, life yours would tell or sing.'

This prince did beg, then plead, then beg some more.
Tears his ran they in floods and touched dwarf's heart.
'So brave, such trust, such love. What fate does store
none know. Hope I words mine from futures part.
At yonder fork there three will meet. Now start
and seek your destiny brave prince and pray
words mine were wrong. Climbed he and sat on cart.
Rejoice with you these two will not this day.
So guard back yours or pay. Greed theirs can they not stay

Wrists gripped, eyes bowed, hearts true had met. Now leave
must they and part. So each did turn to face
the days which lay not known. To live, not grieve,
was their pure vow. To seek those two, did race
this prince, whom greed still filled, no love nor grace.
Then meet did they. News his, eyes green, hearts cold,
received. False joy gave they, false smile on face.
This prince was blind to lies from hearts where gold
was their dark love. Now gone from head what dwarf had told.

These three did chance to find a land war torn
and famine bound. To king this prince then gave
the loaf to famine end and sword was sworn
to win that war. 'Young prince gifts yours did save
land mine and people all. Now slain the knave
who war did bring. Heartfelt thanks mine I swear
as I return gifts yours.' Then cheer and wave
did king and all as prince rode out to where
these gifts, this loaf and sword not once but twice did share

These three to harbour came. A ship did board
for home and king. This prince, so tired, did sleep.
Now two an evil plan did hatch. Afford
no sleep could they. To sleeping prince did creep,
take flask, take gift, with brine, fill flask, then keep
this prince's gift, hard won, for king to heal.
Now sleep these two did take. Two beasts did leap
in nightmare dreams their hearts of black to steal.
So dark hearts theirs, minds theirs, no remorse they could feel.

At dawn did ship in harbour home drop sail
and princes three rode home. This prince, dwarf's word,
recall did he when gift to king did fail
and king was worse not healed. When brothers heard
this prince took they to dungeon deep. Interred
was he and silence sworn or death would meet.
Flask theirs showed they. Now words of dwarf so stirred
such pain in sorrow's loss. Love his, so sweet,
like ring, now gone. This prince, kept hope, so heart would beat.

These two then flask did give to king and cheered
as health returned once more. But dark their lies
in father's ear as tales wound they and jeered
as traitor inferred they. 'This prince now dies!'
This king declared, 'To secret wood,' then cries,
' Oh hunter step now forth! Take bow and son
where none can see and him shoot dead!' Surprise
on hunter's face did show. No tears did run
down father's cheeks. ' Back be before the setting sun!'

With weary heart these two rode out with bow
to hunt the deer. 'Friend mine ,' This prince did say.
'Smile yours and talk all gone this day?' 'To know
what I must do before the end of day.
It grieves soul mine.' This hunter sighed. 'Did pray
that fate would change this path. Sense I that greed
and lies have fooled our king for him to stray
from love for you who rescued two in need
of help. The price is death. Cannot do I this deed.'

'Friend mine, betrayed am I. Now I recall
a warning I no heed did give. But trust
that brother's love was true, like mine. But all
the time, what I have done, their greed it must
them drive to hate. Love mine cast they in dust
and mud. A trifle toy, hearts dark , this heart
sought they to kill. No love for king. A gust
from hell has them entombed. This deed, to start
must you, or you from life our noble king will part.'

Flow

'Prince mine, still true, no angry word, for king
who death commands for you. What loss do see
if deed do I. So no! What proof to bring
to fool both king and sons and you set free?'
Sat they and thought as sun reached top of tree.
'Clothes mine and horse to you give I, now go
or time our plan undoes. Now I do flee
to forest green. These proofs, greed theirs, now know
will their doubts ease. Death mine assured. Blood none will flow'

Then wrists gripped each, a ray of hope did feel
as they now turned to leave. The robes, a deer
on saddle born. Shots two were made. So real
this story looked. So arrow count no fear
would hunter know. Down prince's cheek a tear
did fall as he then slipped away. The sun
in perfect place for their deceit. No ear
had heard, nor eye had seen. So start to run
down tracks, and hide, did he. Now all the world he'd shun.

'Tis done king mine.' The hunter lied and threw
the robes on step of throne. 'Horse his , now tied,
with groom does rest.' 'Friend mine, know I so true.'
This king replied. 'Grief yours is clear'. Outside
this horse did kick and rear. Once master's pride
this steed of white. 'Teach I that nag it's place!'
Did spit a prince. But king forbade the ride.
Then sullen son, green eyed, and sneer on face,
agreed, then smiled, 'Of course, too soon, to soon, your grace.'

Flow

To waiting dwarf a princess ran, 'It's true,
came he my heart to win. So long the wait.
Back home ride I for him, gold path will strew
from road to gate. Then he will ride, so straight
for me will come! Oh dwarf. One thing, so great
joy mine, did I forget to ask. Why I
here was?' This dwarf did smile, 'Would you be late?
The story long would take. Now you should fly
back home and build road yours. Not long till he comes nigh.'

Smiled she then laughed. 'Never do you e'er change.
But father, pleased will be what once, for me,
did you. So farewell dwarf this road arrange
will I.' Down path rode she, 'Good luck,' grinned he.
The king rejoiced at her return, could see
the work was done. 'A debt, this dwarf, do owe.
This road now build. For prince that did set free,
a wife of you may make.' A ball will throw
and you will dance. My blessings great with you will go.

So far away this prince knew not this scene
but starts to think. 'A fool am I to weep,
to sit and mourn loss mine in forest green.
Now clothes have I, a steed, a sword. Not steep
this road to take. For love, ride I, no sleep
will take. Oh Dwarf so right were you back there
and fool was I. Heart mine is true, so creep
not I, nor hide from view from evil heir.
Love mine, no ring to show but I now ride, still care'.

Flow

Green eyed, back home, each son did vie for bride
not known. The first rode he to road of gold.
Kept he steed his on grass to gate. In side
a voice said ,'No!' So home rode he and told
plight his . So second son did ride, not bold,
but cold was he. This road of gold this knight
did leave. On path of stone, like he so cold,
this gate sought he in vain. 'No No! Not right!'
This son returned. No wife. The ring hid they from sight.

The king, while sons were gone, received three gifts
from far away. With thanks came they for deeds
once done by son now dead. King's heart now shifts
from hate to grief, knew he, these two, whose needs
of gold could blind eyes his and mind. 'What seeds
there grew, such greed?' Sighed he. 'King mine, not dead!
Lied I,' the hunter cried. ' Grief yours now leads
heart mine to speak. Son yours to death did lead,
but kill him I could not. On block place I this head.'

'Rise up, Rise up old friend, friend dear . Betray
this king did you. Heart yours was right not wrong.
Send riders bards with words to find this day
son mine so wronged by kith and kin. The throng
must know the truth. Bards mine now write this song.
A foolish king, this mighty son did save
from death, then spurned was he now gone too long.
Go sing this song and beg this son so brave
with bride to come. His brothers two will I enslave!'

Flow

This prince rode he to golden road. Not right
nor left strayed he. This gold meant naught. For heart
sought he and straight to gate flew he. At sight
of her, wept he with joy.' Oh none will part
love mine from you,' The priest, 'Oh king, let's start
vow theirs is made for all to hear!' then cried.
'Quite right, this prince and bride have felt love's dart.
Bless I this day, this prince, now son and bride
are one!' 'Amen!' both priest and all those there replied.

A bard then came from far away. 'A song
have I to share.' Then words went they from mind
'Prince mine, this song, it tells of you. How wrong
father yours feels. Begs he, if you so kind,
can forgive his done foolish deeds. So blind
was he.' The king, now watched this prince, now son.
'Loved I my king, of course come we!' And signed
with seal a letter then. Now bard, do run
to king and him bring here to join this wedding fun!'

'Before leave you add I my seal.' The king
did rise and say. 'This prince watched I and heart
is true. A son of whom am proud. Please bring
king yours so he too share this time and start
to make two kingdoms one. In haste depart.
On your return new song, pray I, will write
of love not lost but true. Earn you this part,
with speed now bring this news to king. This night
when all are met sing you tale yours of restored right.

Sons two returned. Sensed they a change. Too late
    try run did they as angry king was faced.
No sorrow their words filled nor eyes. But wait
    would they to flee. Then news from bard who'd raced
    to tell this king son his was found. These braced
    themselves for death. Now fear, not greed, in eyes
    did show. In dungeon deep were cast. 'Now taste
    death yours will you on return mine. Such lies
wove you, no mercy shown at you death yours now flies.'

So king, with bard and court with haste did head
    for chance to see this prince so wronged yet true,
    who king cast out in bitter haste deemed dead.
    In dungeon deep a plan did creep.' Now you
    and I must think and work this night. For flew
    our crow of death so close. Have we three days
    to plot and flee to lands who know not you
    and I.' These sons so cunning found their ways.
But price to pay? To work in fields till dying days.

Two kings now met with prince and bride. 'So our
    two kingdoms joined with king and queen so rare.'
    The son and father cried in joy. 'This flow'r
    won you now daughter mine. Now bard, words fair
    now sing this tale for all to hear. No care
    do take o'er my role dark. Let all men hear
    how son of mine is true and kind, beware
    the sin of pride.' Sang he so free, with tear,
of prince and bride, water of life and all did cheer.

Flow

How came these princes four to sit, not free
nor know no thing, nor act when prince did stare?
Their tale did start so long ago. Now see
here must begin this tale of kingdom fair.
A king so old, sons fools, not fit, no care
to rule. Their king was wise for all . Like flame
lit he the way. For all shield his was there
to guard and save. His heart of love the same
for all. Spoke he like sword so sharp as truth his aim.

So four called he, 'Now I am old all know.
Uncle now rules and trains sons mine till die
must I and leave rule his in place. Now go
and learn this craft. When you are fit to try,
aside step he, then watch and wait and eye
will know the truth. These sons agreed to wait
and learn. No greed or malice here. The die
was cast. The king did die, wept they. Their fate
now lay in uncle's hands who knew a true king's trait.

Soon he despaired sons' progress slow. They tried
but hopeless they. So he a plea sent out
for wiser help than he. So many plied
their skills in vain. Till dwarf came he about
this place knew he. ' A quest, have I no doubt
would four wise kings produce. 'Oh yes that's right!
With you go they and kings return!' Did shout
this weary uncle who now smiled. 'Tonight
with dwarf ride you with speed to find inside king's light.'

So rode these four with dwarf unknown to where
not known. This dwarf would answer not their pleas
but rode in silence loud. No talk to share.
These four let thoughts and cares twist mind from ease,
till dark vague shapes filled sky, then mist, then trees
possess which rip then flail and fill with dread
the minds of princes four. Whilst dwarf just sees
a track, some trees, and rides at ease. Instead
of fear a track sought he, as readied he a wand and bread.

When track spied he raised hand to halt this ride
to warn these four of branches low and track
of rock and mud. Was slow this way to hide
dark castle great. Which loomed ahead. Not back
these four could flee as path behind in black
was cloaked, no light to lead but on to gate
which, locked against both friend and foe, no crack
it showed for key to turn. These four now wait
for dwarf to speak or clue to give or tell their fate.

Two loaves, a wand of iron strong now shown
to princes four. 'With wand strike gate times three..'
These four did wand then try to grab. Quite thrown
was dwarf at childish bicker and could see
the uncle's plight. 'Let lots be drawn!' Spoke he
in voice that all obeyed. Once lots were drawn
pulled he out loaves. But one held back, to free
the king within did he begin. No pawn
in youth's so fickle games. No loaves from dwarf were torn.

Flow

'Loaves two and iron wand give I to you.
Times three strike you on iron gate then throw
straight way, loaves these to fierce lions two
who wait for those who enter there. Next go
with haste through room of thrones. Int'rest don't show
but pass by there as quest so many lost
in room of thrones. Then all courtesy know
for maiden fair then pass to door. The cost
to those who linger there are hearts and eyes of frost.

To solve the riddle door and cross to where
stand I is your task first. If kings will be
must you not fail. This quest now starts. Beware!
No game is this but life or death. So free
the king within or die. So find the key
to riddle door. So use this wand and bread
and start your quest and soon meet me by tree.'
Then dwarf did point at looming gate. His head
then turned. 'Knocks three, loaves two, a door. With care now
tread'

At dwarf, then steeds, then gate these four did stare.
The dwarf thanked they then gate was struck with wand
times three and loaves then thrown to lion pair.
Then four looked back. No dwarf, nor steeds. Not fond
of work nor war these four, in fear, did bond
as one as gate passed they . On hilts did hands
now rest then shake as gate did slam. Respond
did they with sudden haste to room where stands
not one but four carved thrones once brought from distant lands.

Flow

With haste, this room, left they as dwarf had bade
to do. Then voice so sweet did call and sing
and maiden fair did step in view. Dismayed
that four, not one, had come. So stay, gold ring
on finger slim would do. 'Some quest did bring
all you this way. This work must you now do
as I my own must seek. Of prince, a king,
one day, am I to make,' smiled she then through
a door, unseen by four, like arrow keen she flew.

'What now?' asked eldest prince love struck. 'The door!'
cried he, who'd learnt from lots and loaf. 'To try
the quest of one, when four, is lost. The door,
the door, the door!' 'Too young! Do you know why
that girl and I have met?' 'Of course,' did sigh
this youngest prince. 'The dwarf', said he, 'did say
courtesy know to maiden fair. Not lie
now I!.' 'Her's I, she mine!' 'No I now pray
keep four or none. This dwarf, warned he ,not kings? Death's
prey!'

But three, love struck outnumbered one. 'Let's sit
and talk this out.' said three. 'Not thrones are these
but chairs so tired and worn.' 'Love blinds, so pit
now waits with gaping mouth.' So youngest sees
and sighs. 'The quest is lost. What hope have these
of sight or ear? Fear I no kings reside
in us brothers dear mine . Oh we'll not please
this dwarf, nor king or maiden fair. Not tried,
hard we, so birth now stillborn kings as dead inside!'

Flow

'Too harsh, too harsh! Come sit with us. No frost
can you now see.!' 'That frost will come if I
on chair do sit. Explain to me, now lost,
this girl so fair. Of spring, dawn's air, to my
poor senses she did speak.' 'Of summer's sky
and solstice sun mean you?' ' Of autumn gold
and lakes of rest,' to me. 'You fools! now try
to see, as eldest, right am I. To fold
our quest, is winter's role. Win I for I am bold!'

With heavy heart and steps of dread this king
unborn did sit on thrones of frost. Now four
were filled and curse arose. Slept they. Till ring
of gate did close on heel of he who saw
these stare and almost failed in bed which four
had missed. Bed cursed like thrones. Test his not theirs'.
In darkness now did they awake which tore
the loss of time now spent on frozen chairs
now warm. The blood on gate had freed, once more, these heirs.

So slow, so slow did they now try to wake
both mind and body cold from stupor deep.
No thoughts nor mem'ry rose to help or take
their minds to where were they or why. This sleep,
this curse, did seep, where ghosts nor fears won't creep.
No I, to focus on this mind did pray
for anchor strong to ground on reef then leap
on sand, then stone then land. To stand and say,
'free I from curse now stand, thanks give for sight this day.'

'Dreams mine, of bear, were full,' the eldest son
declared. 'Of eagle strong,' the youngest sighed.
'Rode I on salmon's fin.' 'With stag did run
in dreams did I.' These four to self who lied
then sighed, 'So we are where, oh yes, such pride
did us lead here.' Young prince, no king, did lay
this weighty truth on all. 'So dark!' then cried.
'Not dark!' a cracked aged voice, coldly, did say.
In quest, failed you, not dead, but second chance this day.'

'Another came, heart pure, for she, who you
did waste thoughts yours of love and try to gain.
There's light enough but you don't see. It's true
that darkness lies behind the eyes. So train
eyes yours and mind to see. This truthful grain
now you must grasp, and see. In dark is light,
in light is dark. So choose, now know, or pain
in you will hold tight you to loss. Now plight,
for you, is choice so choose. Stay blind or free right sight.'

'If kings are you, and princes not, this quest
now needs to start. For uncle's old so choose,
with care, path yours . Let mind be wisdom's guest.
That blood on floor reminder be. To lose
this quest, not find in you a king will bruise
a father's dreams. If uncle dies then some
will come and take what should be yours. So who's
this fool, who'd lose crown theirs, when strangers come?
On scales now rest this quest and your father's kingdom.'

Flow

Then rose, these four, as aching joints did cry
as cold was warmed by rubbing hands. Then turn,
as one to blood on gate. A pad, then eye
of lion turned, then tongue, did seek to learn
and lick the taste of life not death. To churn
inside did four so close to death who'd been.
As minds did clear, knew each role theirs, now stern
did faces set. This king within not keen
before now rose in heart. These crowns in minds now seen.

Then table laid saw they then minds snapped back.
'Here we had purpose lost in mist of time?'
Young prince for all did speak, 'As fools did lack
king's hearts and minds.' As girl recalled through grime
of minds did flit and soar. 'Such fools!' did chime
these four. Table for four was laid saw they.
Now stale, long dried a feast long cold. Of thyme
a hint in air now stale. Their quest, the way
to free the king within did hint. 'now don't delay.'

As stir, then walk these four, 'That's it, the door,
where first came she to us.' 'Not door to quest
of yours,' cracked voice began. Beware of your
chance last that hangs by thread so slim to test,
reveal the king, or not perhaps. No rest
for you fear I.' These four, found bed, did stare,
'So huge, for who? But we best leave for guest
it's for,' spoke eldest son, 'not I cold chair
would live again.' 'Learn you at last,' spoke dwarf so rare..

Flow

'See I more light from where? Lamps none. No sky
through window seen.' One prince did point to wall
so dark.' 'In time, this light, so clear, your eye,
then mind will grasp. Here learn, no fiery ball,
or sphere of silver, sky does light or call
the times of day or night. Now see yon door
in arch of stone. No key, old oak, to all
is clear. To gain place yours with me be sure
to think as kings not fools or stay for evermore.'

Charged prince at door, then paused did he, and look,
then point at symbol'd door. These four, this sight
of those in dreams last seen did haunt, then shook
the king within to stir and think. 'Not might
need we. It seems, dreams ours of four in night,
so cold, were keys. Now each their creature sought.
an eagle, stag, then salmon, bear when light
so strange did change symbol to stone. Now naught
to lose these stones were pressed. 'A crack, a creak' ears caught.

Through open door passed four then stood amazed.
'A wood? In castle deep?' Eldest exclaimed.
'No sun, yet bright as day!' said he now dazed
by sights unseen till now. One track, low framed,
now called. With boughs of blooms and thorns sharp aimed
at those who careless pass. These four did bend
and stumble much. No curse from lips defamed
this quest begun at last. But each, its end
did sense not close. Asked one,' would fate be foe or friend?'

Then path did end in clearing large. Deep pool
so still did greet the eyes, surprised, so wide.
To drink or bathe tired limbs in water cool
was their desire. 'No cup?' says one. Then chide
these four did dwarf now seen. ' At last decide
to seek this quest have you begun. At door
first task passed you .The cup, not yours, did ride
with one, like you, who almost failed. Ignore
words mine, then fail do all as you, so plainly, saw.

To bathe in pool is not for you a choice.
Come tell to me why you are here.' Then stared,
at dwarf, at pool, these four, then sat. No voice
could find. But think did they when light then flared
in mind and eyes. As one rose they then shared
with dwarf quests four.' An eagle calls from east
to me,' The youngest prince, not scared, now dared
to pose. Then each their quest did state. At least
this hope which rose, like sword of dawn, slew doubt like beast.

Then eyes to dwarf raised they. Stones four and steeds
there stood. No horse like these, these four had seen.
Stared they as these, to drink in pool, dwarf leads.
One red, one white, one black, one blue yet green.
Each knew, though none been told, which steed did mean
each prince to ride. If dwarf did grin was hard
to tell. 'Succeed, will we?' asked one. As lean
on trunk of oak did dwarf. 'A future's marred
by past of those whose future 'tis. So face fates' card.'

Flow

So stones were laid on horses back. Then mount
did four with faces fixed on quest once more.
Then each did vow to meet again and count
the days till then. 'Return as kings or four
will lie on earth and rot. In mind be sure
and clear and trust your father's hopes not tears.'
This dwarf in somber tones did state.' Now four
had learnt the words of dwarf to heed and ears,
this time, alert to words prepared to face quest's fears.

Did salute them and wish them well but smile
withheld as four did leave. This dwarf did rest
and gaze in pool to watch these four. Awhile
would four on path be gone. But they, of quest,
not theirs, but his, knew not. In stones did nest
a secret deep now born on horse's back.
This dwarf did smile, now close to end of test
which long ago, for him, began. How black
the days, the nights the years. 'Let four not courage lack.'

The gift in dwarf was sight, much trust and time.
So long ago to council called when young
was dwarf. The days were dark in hope when grime
of doubt and fear were sown. The bards they sung
no songs of joy but loss of common tongue.
Spoke tree to beast or nymph to men in hall
of oaks where none were feared and trust seemed hung
in heart and mind. And four would come to call
of oak. Left they their home in star and sun for all.

These four, on wings which lay on face, on back
and heels, would bring to all symbol and sign
from stars, from those beyond so none would lack
in knowing all were bound as one. Divine
through time and space a spark in all. No line
between, but through, joined all to all. All shared
and grew as speech was clear, and light did shine
flowed love then strength in life and death. Life flared
so bright in hall of oak where all by all well fared.

From where or when, from sight of all, a dark
and heavy shadow rose, so doubt and fear
began to scar the trust in all. Its mark
like wall split sprite from men and beast then steer
the nymphs from trees. 'So where the four?' did jeer
a voice unseen. The four, who saw and heard
a council called in hall of oak where seer
did speak so clear. These four with gifts did gird
this hall. 'These stand 'gainst doubt and fear. As bond, our word.'

'But comes the day, when signs are gone, dear friends.
In truth these signs are here to counter doubt
and fear. No home is this for them. Now ends
a time and starts a change, Within, not out,
of heart and mind these signs need be. To rout
these days some time will take. False priests will say
through them, alone, a way exists and shout
that truth, one way, is theirs. In time, a ray
will rise and one descend to end this change one day.'

While some did seek to trust once more and talk
did nymph to man and beast to bird. A line
now fell, not through, between for some so walk
no more as one would they. No trust in sign
or word of four. In fear and doubt did pine
in heart and mind for something lost once known.
To sign would they not go on foot, decline
in dreams to touch. No more would they intone
or chant of light divine. but grew a heart of stone

Then dwarf recalled the day, dark day, word came.
To council he was called in hall of oak.
So young, back then, in doubt was he.,' Not shame
on me now put.' His father's words then broke
the doubt. 'If called are you, then go,' and spoke
not stern or harsh but smile at son so young
but known. This smile, heart his and mind, did stoke
up trust, not doubt. 'Now use wit yours and tongue,
with trust and time as wise are you,' as father sung.

So dwarf to council rode through lands so dark
with fear. A somber mood o'er council laid
like ash from earth thrown fire. These few did mark
the last who walked as one. Here sprite, afraid
was not of men, nor beast, nor nymph and stayed
these few, still stood against this dark, still cared
to keep in mind divine within. But frayed
were they as dwarf did sit. 'The signs, once shared,
are gone. Now change, as warned, has come these few despaired.'

Flow

'So dwarf, to you turn we. These signs, from four
return, must you, to them. The who and where
is lost to us.' Then words once said before
returned. 'No shame on me do put.' Aware
was dwarf, as words did form in mind, that care
and time would stand him well. Bowed he, then left.
No words to say, no breath to waste. 'Who'd dare
to take the signs?' thought he , then laughed. The theft,
the thief, was waste of thought. To where, his mind, he cleft.

The time it passed so slow for those in hall
of oak. That dwarf returned success implies?
Smiled dwarf, 'The who and how these signs did fall
to hands is known but these leave I. These eyes
have seen the where. So now, with leave, now rise
shall I, to rescue signs, need I a thief,'
winced he. But trust was law, so no surprise,
in hall of oak at words of dwarf. Relief
it flowed. So dwarf then left for girl, was strong belief.

Some months rode he in search of one who'd show
a skill so scarce. Unseen by those from whom
stole she. Not sleight of hand would she e'er know.
From forest deep did dwarf emerge. To groom
steed his did he then pause. On road, did loom
ahead, a castle dark on hills of green.
So dwarf and steed did walk that way. No room
for haste or rush. For time was key. Serene
the mind and sharp as sword. Walked slow, to gate, now seen.

Flow

      Past guards and noise, then paused by stall. But shoved
           aside was he. This place, so cold, as low
    saw dwarves and all who odd did seem. Not loved
  was steed nor beast who served. The dark, did know,
     and fear, too well, this place. But one, did show
          a spark of care. 'Now you! Apologise
        to dwarf for knock!' A face, did try, of foe
      their fear to lose. Of her or dwarf, his eyes
not clear quite who this fear inspired. This dark spreads lies.

   To dwarf, turned girl,. 'Princess,' bowed he. 'To king,
     and father old, go we. For he dwarves knew,
    says he.' Then paused, did she. 'Wear I, no ring,
      no dress of gold, this day. Is keen and true
     this mind of yours. So rare 'tis seen in few.'
    This king in garden sat and smiled at friend
     of daughter wild of his. 'So dwarf, who's new
       to me, come you at time well met.' 'To end
this dark, no doubt, are you a key, think I, to mend.'

     As dwarf to speak began. 'Oh no!' with hand
    on head this king did cry as Prince, now red
   with anger strode ,'Ring mine! The best in land,
   now sits in nest long cold. Times three now said
      so leave will I. Young princess, sir, in bed
  said she, then town, now here. Ring mine, in nest,
    'twas her know I. Not her, no sir, not wed
     her I. Plays she, like thief unseen. 'tis best
leave I this night. So sir! Times three, warned I, no jest.'

Flow

This king, once ring returned and prince long gone,
to dwarf did turn. 'Was she with us, were eyes
deceived? The truth she spoke, think I. This done
times oft. So now, doubt I, a queen now lies,
nor wife, in child of mine.' Sad king then sighs.
In mind of dwarf thought he of her observed
at play. 'What's seen, my king, know I, belies
the truth. Know I that quests, by men, are served.
At question mine, my king, now friend, be not unnerved.'

'This child, friend mine, this daughter dear, not wed
will she. The court is tired of trick and prank.
When suitors rich do fall and faint, 'tis said,
that yawns does she, so bored. So none do thank
for prize so rich. 'If catch, they can, then rank
of mine are they, when play do I.' says she
'but lose do they, no rank of mine, so bank
up pillow mine would they? No I, stay free!'
To question yours nod I. To quest do I agree.'

'If queen and bride return to me then go
with blessings mine. If fail do you, as all
have done before, this dark has won and know
no bride in her resides. No child will call
to her, 'mother, watch me, on horse so tall.'
This king did call to princess child, then say,
'With dwarf now ride. Find bride and queen. Don't stall
this quest. With blessings mine on you this day
to ride with dwarf whom I need you to trust, obey.'

Flow

So king then watched from castle wall as two
did leave that day. From keep did seep some dark
as light was felt by all. One gift, he who
this dwarf had pushed, did give. Keen hawk to mark
the day long gone when he with dwarf did hark
when prey was dead. When ride and talk all could
with sprite and nymph and beast. A lark
then rose. Its song then sung, flew it in wood
unseen. Till far from sight the king still waved, then stood.

This dwarf and precocious young girl did ride
through night or day. 'How strange smell you?' Spoke she.
This dwarf did pause and wait. Thoughts his did hide
so deep. 'How good, at game now seen,' thought he
'are you? This quest will test both you and me.'
'Of what?' a sigh gave he. 'I, false sigh, think?
'Not sure.?' grinned he. 'Of what? ask I of thee.'
'Of earthen ore but something more on brink
of mind and tongue. Like steam? 'Twixt earth and you, a link?'

This dwarf did grin once more. 'That's good, how good
at game that you do play? Too fast for eye
to see. Observe did I and saw. Most would
then keep what steal they do, not you. So why
so steal, then keep not prize? A game to try
and see? But what? Own you, young girl, a gift!'
This dwarf did laugh and chuckle loud then sigh.
'Quest yours begins and hard will be as sift
this gift and you to full to test how well, unseen, you lift.'

Flow

'So where, and why, are we to go this day?'
A pause, then dwarf in eyes of girl did stare.
'To see if queen resides in here,' did say
the dwarf with hand on heart, 'and south.' 'To where?
The south! The lands of heat!' 'Try not to care
of names too much. Hot Lands so called, but I
have found don't fear a name until you share
its space. Of course with caution walk when nigh.
Then trust the gift within not just what's seen by eye.'

'But why go south? Please tell to me.' 'This gift
and father's hopes. To steal from they who stole.'
'To steal?' laughs she, 'To steal, how strange, to lift
unseen, a thing, is rare request to dole
to me as father disapproved this role
in court. A queen, who steals, rare queen indeed.
But I may not desire , this 'thing', our goal.'
'That ring took you but kept it not. No greed
have you, desired to keep not once. The theft's your need.'

To south did go this dwarf and thief as heat
did grow intense. Hot sun, dry dust, did choke
and catch the breath with every step and beat,
heart hers, in pain, did throb in chest and stoke
the fire within.. 'Human, am I, but broke
by heat and strain. To steal, must I, soon rest.'
Then dwarf did look. No heat, felt he, not poke
flesh his. 'As steam and ore, no sweat.' was guessed,
'through skin, could pierce. But me, this heat could end our quest.'

Flow

As she, down sat, and grime did wipe from face
did dwarf agree, 'Some help, think I now need.'
Sound strange, made he, a song, so old, did grace
this land once more. In her it stirred a seed
which she then felt root take. A sleeper freed
inside did wake as kissed by song like charm.
Did Mother rise then stand beside with creed.
'Not all is all, nor none is none, stay calm,
Nor light is light,nor dark is dark safe you from harm.'

'This gift have we, that I concealed, in life,
to take a thing, unseen, by all. Survive,
could you. But trust gets lost. The cost is strife
then doubt. King yours, my love, so wise, did strive,
for love of me and you, to teach. 'Like hive,
be one in all and trust.' Kissed 'wake by song
both you and I now talk. So hard, when five,
lost you my breath, king yours still cries, so long,
in sleep for me. The queen in you awakes, be strong.'

Gift yours, not thief, but more. So wake now child,
this time, so brief, is yours. As kiss give I,
not cold, but warm. This dwarf, know I, once wild,
tamed gift of his. So watch, then learn, don't lie,
as sleeping. Wake. That song, sang he, did my
death pause, life yours, so meet could we once more.
But time now fades this song for us. Don't try
just be. If try, all fail. Be strong and sure.
Helps nigh to those who despise not a gift so pure.'

Flow

To dwarf turned she, 'This thing that we do seek
have you not told to me its shape or kind.
To know of this some help would be but speak
not you on this.' 'Of what you speak you'll find
and know full soon.' spoke dwarf with face then lined
in thought as iron wand on ground did land.
Then gentle pad heard she of paw, behind,
'What's that?' As she did stare wide eyed, 'So grand,
this creature I've ne'er seen back home which close does stand!'

'A lion she which called, did I, to aid
and carry us to where this treasure hides.
There you can plan and think then lift what's laid
unseen by eyes but mine. Walks she where tides
of heat and dust do hide prey hers. These prides
through haze perceive need theirs. Then swiftly take
the life then feed. Last time came I two rides
gave she so way is known. Tis time to break
the deeds of thieves whose arts will you now seek to shake.'

'So mount on back of her do we. This heat
of ground, those paws, not harms for she, pads thick,
each day these ways does stalk then lie. To meet
your future we must leave.' 'If I, not sick
with heat would excited be. This fur does stick
and prick yet soft to touch is she.' The way
through lands so hot was easier made. When crick
her neck this girl did then as turn to say
and point as mount of fire did loom not far away.

'Is that the place where we do head to steal
from mount of fire?' This day, fear I, much pain
will come.' 'Not fear, but trust must you, and feel
the gift within soon rise.' Old dwarf again.
did grin. 'For queen to rise let me explain.
Not eas'ly earn what I, through quest, to you
do give.' Stared she, transfixed across that plain
at fiery mount which thundered, roared, did spew
rocks red, clouds grey. Learn trust in dwarf, must she now knew.

'Roasted will I by fire and soon in pit
of boiling rock and steam!' 'This think about
must you now do.' 'But how will I, if wit
is found, then know this thing to lift, bring out,
for you?' 'Of this will you have soon, no doubt.'
Then dwarf did whistle strange, then answer shrill
from high in sky where eagle paused, did shout,
then dived, so swift. Then clutched was she. So still,
did she then be, for fear of fall felt she not thrill.

Then voice of one did rise again. 'To trust.
must you the queen within.' So far below
peered she in fire and steam, pool red, hot dust.
'So hot,' says she, 'what's that, a glimpse, too low
in pit for me to clearly see or know?
Then picture crept in mind from eagle's eye
so sharp. 'A cup, too special. Who would throw
this wondrous jew'l in pit of fire to lie
unseen? This art of fools undo but how do I?'

Flow

Now nearer flew this mighty king of sky.
'This dust it chafe's and burns!' thought she, 'Now sad.
if fail, die I. At news will father cry.
That cup blame I when tears weeps he, so bad
a thief am I,' wept she. Now clouds, Thor mad,
did build then clap and hail, hard rain did pelt
from sky which roared and flashed. 'So now, here clad,
in clothes so soaked this quest hate I.' So dealt
her hate like cards, at fate, like ice, so cold it felt.

This rain and hail did snow become. This storm
now filled the desert sky. Too cold to care
watched she and stared when eagle dived. To form
a plan no time as steam, grew cold. Aware,
this bird, as rocks did cool, then swoop to where
this cup, was hid, Now she, hands free, could lift
the prize from mount subdued. So cold, this pair,
but eagle soared to clearer sky. A gift
uncalled by voice did rise within. 'Warm air cold shift!'

Then down to waiting dwarf flew it as mount
did flame and roar once more. Did she farewell.
to noble king of sky then bid. 'From fount
of fire, cup yours, give I.' 'If one did tell
what just befell that snow in hot lands fell
which quenchedand froze the mount believe their talk
not I.' spoke dwarf ,'of lies, this tale, would smell,'
as cup in bag placed he. Now lion did walk
till farewells made and she once more her prey could stalk.

Flow

Now deep inside a queen had stirred. 'There's three
like cup for you to lift from thieves now know.'
Sighed she, 'as horrid place as mount?' 'Maybe,
but yes, expect as bad.' This dwarf did show
no care yet grin again did he. 'So go
where next?' asked she. 'Go we the way we are.'
'Guess I, as south behind it's north to snow?'
'Bright girl!' 'Do you simple call me?' 'No. Far
go we so plans of thieves the gift in you will mar.'

To north, so cold, rode they this cold did seep
and creep inside. 'Not far from home are we
our kingdom's cold.' 'Oh yes but not so deep
as this fear I.' Then she could feel and see
agreed did she. Then dwarf did pause by tree
and cloaks of bearskins two from bag did take.
'Of this warm fur so glad am I.' Then he
did nod as on went they. Then snow did make
the way so hard, 'No break, till we, though slow, reach lake.'

'Wants who the cup that I did lift and why
and what still fills cup rare?' So he it took
in cup did look. 'Hmmm.' he did shrug and sigh.
Still frozen. He in bag placed cup. Then look
to stars, then way ahead. Shrugged he. No book
to guide plans his or ways. This dwarf ahead
so straight his route did take. Laughed he then shook
the snow from fir and hood. Gave he some bread
to her to warm the blood. For soon on ice would tread.

By frozen lake, a hut long cold, where steeds
were left in stable full of straw for where
path theirs would lead to walk must they. 'It leads
to where unfair, a steed, to ride.' Then share
some broth by hasty fire. Then leave, no care
for sleep so close were they. Path theirs, so hard
became. The cold did bite and sting. But fare
well them these bearskin cloaks so warm. But barred
the way oft tried downed trees. Dwarf's axe, did hack to shard.

To frozen sea came they where crystal waves
did over hang from time once warm. 'This land
of ice, not ice but stone. 'tis wrong. Behaves
as sea by winter caught in time. But stand
now we on ice that lies below. Not hand
nor foot deceived but eye, 'spoke she as stone
in crystal form stroked she. 'By who's command
this ice to stone transformed?' Iceberg, alone,
in distance loomed as snow did whirl where wind did moan.

Then full surprise on dwarf's old face did show
as girl, with shield, now stood with grin so wide.
For snow and wind had his sight blocked, when go
did she to lift this prize from thieves. No pride
had she o'er skill of hers. 'Did once abide
at home a storyteller wise. 'Not eye
but hand and foot trust you when stood astride
a tricksy place. What is is not. Take my
advice and cover eyes. Then live will you not die.''

Flow

'Words his trust I so shield gained I.' Spoke she
to dwarf who shield in bag did place as storm
did roar and wail in ears, on face. Then he
did point to way from whence came they. To form
in mind a plan did he. But first, to warm,
in hut awhile once tricksy sea had left.
'Have scar, from eye to ear, who you inform
of tricksy place, did he?' asked dwarf, 'Which theft
did aid in crystal sea.' 'Oh yes, and hand so deft.'

By fire, that night, did they then sleep till dawn
did call their quest awake, to ride twice more.
So tired mind from sleep and dreams was torn..
When final two from thieves took she all four,
now safe in bag of dwarf, asked she, 'What law,
is there, that I who stole, no trial face I'
Then dwarf did turn, 'Ask you the queen, now door,
not blocked, within, not I. The right to try
is royal work not mine. Within must you now pry'

Long time rode they till gate reached they. 'This quest
is done?' 'To soon, for you to think of where
came you,' did smile this dwarf. 'For you, a guest,
for time must be.' In hand, rod his, so rare,
to her gave he. 'For you to use, if dare,
so gate will turn on hinge. Then enter in.'
'And how to use?' 'One strike on gate.' 'Then stare,
at rod, did she. 'Just one, not three.' To win
her fate this gate struck she. 'Miss I my kith and kin.'

Flow

As gate did swing two sleeping lions lay.
Then stretch awake and pad to sides of maid
as she then entered in. 'It's bright as day,'
did she exclaim as gates did slam. Then preyed,
on mind once more this quest, so strange, that played
with fate. 'So few, this light do see so soon.
A question I now sense. Father yours prayed
as queen would you return from quest and boon
for queen is king.' Husband! Ne'er I o'er man will swoon.'

This dwarf, so wise, to press not her did grin.
Then stare did she then point at thrones which stood
in line austere and table spread, not thin,
for feast not held. 'Keep well away, for good,
will I from room of thrones. A spell in wood
does lurk unseen sense I.' As leave, did they,
this haunted room. Then pass through way that could
by few be seen and claimed that room for stay,
hoped she, not long. In awe, watched she, as light did play.

Then riddle door did she then spy, ' Oh these
are easy play for thief. But bed beside
this door, so long and wide not here to please
as sheets, like thrones, have hidden curse inside.'
Through door went dwarf and she who cried
in joy, 'This wood is larger in than out!'
Strange cup did dwarf reveal. Its patterns lied
in weave and dance in glaze. Eyes hers, no doubt
did show. 'Like me it seeks its home. 'Tis hereabout.'

'Its home, my quest, no doubt,' as cup in hand
was placed. Then dwarf did nod 'Be wise, with care
this final quest make you. On ancient land
does this wood stand. Its rules and laws, not fair
to us seem they. What lurks and hides won't share
its home with cup. Now he with scar from ear
to eye of this will he have told to scare
with warnings deep. For he and I did fear
first meet when here we walked, both young, too full of cheer.'

Down twisted path did she move swift and light.
No thorns did catch nor branches snag. Ahead
a pool in clearing lay. To top, for sight,
a tree climbed she. Then catch a view which fed
mind hers with doubt. The pool, cup's home, instead
there lived an ancient beast of which now known
who's eye its' venom wore not fang. This said,
not long was she in ancient land. As hone
skills hers from tales of old learned she at foot of crone.

To dwarf who stood alone did she return.
'That beast, in dreams so dark, have fought oft I
with mirror close to hand. Did watch and learn
as beast, at play, did ripple pool so eye
no venom ply to self. Beast fight not try
would I but cup in pool in silence placed.
This cup does rule dark pool and beast did cry
as patterned cup then mirrored stillness traced
and venomed eye itself espied so death was faced.'

Flow

'Pained writhings, twistings, piercing screams filled air
as trees round pool were felled and beast to stone
then dust became and baselisk did share
this mortal world no more with none to moan
nor weep, nor watch its death, so slow, alone
apart from I who watched, heart cold. Then pool
at edge the cup on bank did place as groan
from forest rose for friends now felled by tool
now dust. Then tears shed I for these by water cool.

Then ravens black their seeds did take. Then rain
of life on distant plain from sky did fall.
As turn to leave did I this groan of pain
a song became. Deep tones of praise did call
to ravens' gift. Then pool did form clouds tall
of water's life which wind, to plain, did bear
where gentle rain then fell on seeds so all
might rise in time from those who fell. To share
this pain and praise taught thief, too cold, in me to care.

Then womb within did stir in hope a dream
of golden path for one to ride then claim
bride his and queen. This quest, so strange, extreme
in test is done for I, on love, once lame
and blind, now wait in peace for one who's name
with mine will join. On quest will be, not me,
but life from pool beyond to seek. No shame
on you will fall in father's eye when see
a queen return to wait for king. Owe you will he.'

Flow

So dwarf by pool, his work nigh done. Did wait
as thoughts of not so distant past did fade
as sun behind green hills in dreams. Quest's fate,
with his, now one. But trust in time still stayed
a friend to mind. No fear, just thoughts which played
and danced, as watch these four, in mirrored pool
by whom a beast was slain. To be dismayed
no trait of his. Rod his a faithful tool,
these waters stirred till east was seen in water cool.

This prince, to east, on steed so white did ride.
Behind back his tongues old did wag and say
tongues two had he. One white one black inside
mouth his. These fought so words of his were grey.
Words his could none e'er trust. So most did pray
no king of theirs would he become. A reign
of grey feared they. If king within, this day,
would rise these tongues must he enslave and train,
through quest, for king inside to rise alive not slain.

In him, not yet, did truth reside as lies
did weave from mouth to ear. So none would dare
word his to cross. For prove, would he, with cries
too loud for truth, that those which heard, no care
ear theirs did take when he did speak. Unfair,
to him were they. The lies were theirs for they
did surely know a prince, no lie in air
would place but truth alone. Now he this day,
alone, did ride and truth did seek to find the way.

Flow

Now forest path grew weak, way hard became
as sword some briars did fail to cut or tear.
For he, the price for sword, agreed not same
as smith recalled. Revenge for lies, not care,
on final edge, this smith, did take. 'Tis rare
to cross a smith. Only a fool would take
the risk, still pay would they when smith unfair
did treat. This fact on prince not lost did make
a curse arise, then pause, as king began to wake.

Then path in clearing ceased. Old man did rest
in huddle grey and cold. At prince did look
in hope, this man. But journey, hard, not best
looked prince in robes now torn. Time he then took,
to speak, this prince, as crumbs of loaf, were shook,
not shared, off cloak. 'Seek I a way, so straight,
to where this journey ends.' A fool, to hook,
with ease,' old man, sly eyed, did think. 'Do wait
for where you head, prince young , this 'where' need you to state.'

With haughty huff, this prince now rough in talk
too gruff did state, 'The east, sunrise, do seek!'
Old man, did pause, then stir. From tree a stalk
broke he. In turf played he then turned to speak.
'This path soon ends and fork will face. So bleak
this place not right or middle take.' This traced
in turf so prince, so clear, could see. Now weak
and tired this prince did nod, thanks none, but raced
to fork now shown. Old man did grin at path prince faced.

Flow

Soon fork in path arose so he left chose.
'Twas straight, too late, old man to thank thought he.
Then bandits fell on him like plague. These rose
from ditch unseen. But sword, for this, once free
from scabbard worn, was cast. These bandits three
did he engage. Mistake made they as eyes
deceived by cloak, so torn, now three did see
a prince was faced. As sword was raised these cries
of chase to flee did change. Hands theirs did take no prize.

Now path so firm to mire did change so steed
through mud was slow as mire did suck and claw
at hoof and thigh. From path so poor be freed
wished steed and prince. Then hope did rise. Before
eyes theirs did rise a path of stone. No more
did steed this mire let victor be. To gain
this place, of spur, no need. As horse from store,
so deep within, this path of stone on plain
did gain. At rain, which fell, to cleanse did none complain.

This path of stone was not as seemed. Hard flint
now struck at hoof and boot as walk, not ride,
on weary steed did prince. This flint, not stint,
on pain free giv'n to foot in boot. To chide
himself for trust in map, old man. No guide
were those. Soon ground did change as softer earth
did comfort hoof and boot. Then pause, not stride
or ride, so horse could graze, restore, as girth
and saddle laid on rocks and king within sought birth.

Flow

Soon prince, steed his, did once more mount to seek
fate his. On nearby stone old man did blow
on flute of reed. 'Lied you to me and speak
so false of way, so straight, where I should go!
Those bandits fierce, then mire, then stone does show
to me no truth from you with me was shared!'
'With you agree can't I. This path, now know,
is straight. From bends and hills is body spared,
as old, am I!' At prince's eyes defiance stared.

'For you did I on path o'ertake this day
then wait.' A grin, by prince unseen, did spread
so scar from mouth to ear did seem to play
on ancient cheek. 'Mind you, prince young, that said,
no horse have I. 'Twas straight and level bed
of ease for I today. For you, 'twas straight
but hard. Same bed young prince. So calm the head
and learn to think on truth and lies or fate
on you'll be hard. So truth not lies did I relate.'

Old man, from prince, then went with grin and wave.
Then prince on words did ponder slow. For lie,
felt he, old man had told. But truth from cave
of trick'ry stood as truth which try deny
did he. To sword, then smith, old man did fly
thoughts his on truth and lies. At home 'grey tongue',
knew he, name his when back was turned. Then try
to turn from quest did he. Head his, low hung,
'No king in I resides!' As stones at path were flung.

But steed some comfort gave and he once more
did mount. A child, did he espy whose tears
and wails did cease as prince appeared. Before
tears hers could she try wipe there came new fears
which darting eyes revealed. 'Beware what rears
beyond this place.' this girl, now bold, did warn.
'What rears and where.?' this girl asked he. 'Has ears,
so sharp they listen now. A hag, not born
to care but beat poor I and dress today has torn.'

'So sir this path should you avoid not take.
This hag, no love, just hate for girls, like me,
or boys and beatings hard.' But prince did make
mind his up quick. 'The hag, risk I, to see.'
Round bend and there a woman old saw he.
Stooped she as apples red in basket placed.
'Old mother you do seem distressed by tree?'
'Attacked by children bold was I. So faced
with loss of winter fruit not I a blow did waste.'

'These children bold could ask of me to share
fruit mine which I would not refuse. But they,
each year, as tribe, descend to taunt, not care,
but steal from tree. No fruit from tree to stay
cold death of winter's grip. No spring's first day
e'er see old I again. So spare this stick
not I when thieves do try to steal and prey
on those deemed old and weak. Send I, to lick
wounds their's each year as learn not they my fruit don't pick.'

Flow

Then prince did help to ease load hers till store
was safe inside. Then girl, again was met.
'Lied you to me!' this prince did state once more.
'Lie I did not!' did girl retort. To set
right her this prince began, 'To me a debt
of truth owe you. Said you this Hag did beat
for nothing done?' This wily child adept
with words case her's then put. This prince took seat
of stone to see eyes hers so clear and voice entreat.

"Tis true the words said I to you. The boys
and I did swoop to take fruit hers. But fared
not well did I not fruit but stick and noise
till fly could I from rod and curse not spared.
No joys of fruit so sweet but wounds not cared
about by she!' This girl did huff then go
down path alone. This prince at girl just stared
and thought. As mount did light in heart now grow.
Truth his and lies, mouth grey of these did he full know.

The sound of water running fast did snap
mind his from thoughts so hard. A river wide
no bridge in sight too deep for steed would trap
quest his on river's edge. By bank did ride
in hope of bridge or ford. Then he espied
a welcome sight of boat, which moored, did cling
to river's edge. A man there stood astride
both bank and boat. 'To cross what coin of king
is paid?' This said, then paid, this boat to prince did bring.

Flow

'The time to cross how long?' asked prince as oar
in water placed. 'As long does take,' replied
this boatman strong. 'But bank not far for sure!
And hurry I am in.' This boat did glide
to stronger flow then row did he. But side,
tho' close, did further get, for to collect
at point agreed in time long gone, so slide
this boat, collect the few, then row. Respect
showed those on board this boat. On this did prince reflect.

Then boat, upstream, when full, to shore was rowed.
'This crossing long by you not told was I?'
'Ask not did you, of time but price. Then showed
did you your gold of king. Your need did die
ignored. As mine, long time, with those didst lie
who bond of trust, of time at place agreed.
Need yours, to cross so swift, not mine. To cry
unfair is prince's lot.' On bank, now freed
from river's flow did nod, agree, then mount white steed.

By distant pool sat dwarf with rod as south
now he did ask this water cool reveal.
This prince in life in choice was weak, with mouth
did speak no truth nor lies. For choice no zeal
had he. Erratic mind of his made feel
unsafe so people feared reign his. Judged he
on merit not nor law of land. To kneel
at foot of one aware of none would see
the kingdom lost thought they and end king's fam'ly tree.

Flow

Times oft, when patrolled borders he, attacked
were castle walls. If king, in prince, did lie
'twas deep unseen or felt by he. This fact
so clear to all was known. Did father try
this king within to bring to surface nigh.
So now this prince on south relied to take
chance last for father's dreams to satisfy.
So sleep could he in grave, not turn. So make
for south in haste did he and speed from dwarf and lake.

As south rode he the air did warm and close
this air became so sweat did he. No care
for sweat as choice of his did mind engross,
to ride, as close, while day its light would share
and steed allow, then path could lead to where
quest his would take. But slow and hard the way,
as forest thick, became. Yet unaware
rode he of cost to cloak and robe. For day
now hot had night so cold for cloak would he then pray.

For king to rise, aware, this prince, did need
become. For scales to work and balance fair,
which weights and facts of law of land and deed
to judge, wise kings well trained, must be aware.
This prince did ride full robed in heat. No care,
to balance facts and need in forest thick
for self did take. So scales did show in air
not straight but tipped, him favoured not, soon trick
of fate this judgement poor his mind would beat with stick.

Flow

Then prince a clearing small did see. Old man
did sit and eat by fork in path. As chew
on flesh fast stuck on bone, from mouth there ran
a stream of red to chin. Then rag not new
wiped he on face and nod at prince. Now few
the words this prince used he. ' Way which is best,
for south to journey fast must I? Know you?'
Then brow in wrinkled thought did crease then rest
as bone did point then pause then point then rest on chest.

This prince did cough, then glare now patience weak.
"Tis me that you did ask of south's road fast ?
Thought I 'boy mad to ask of trees and seek
way fast to south'. So bone did point at last.
'Path right fine is but left have I in past
to south swift trod. Yon' middle path is same
in ease and speed. Could choose from dice now cast?.
If path not liked another take. This game
of choice not hard to play but you, your mind, do maim.'

Then man did grin. Bone cold tossed he then left.
This prince confused by words on game path right
did ride. O'er path did loom rocks large with cleft
for bandit's pole. Then mind did think of night
when these do thieve by pull on pole with might.
Rocks large seal fast prey theirs, like fish in net,
Then swoop do they their prey to slay in fight.
Now prince, feared not this fight. Thought he to let
time his be lost, end then quest young, mind his, did fret.

Returned then he, oft done before, learned not
did he. Down middle path rode prince. But bring
no relief choice now made. Path hard soon got
as steep did rise so back rode he. No king
did stir within. So left rode he. Then ring
did words in mind of paths which question drew.
'Am I such fool time mine now lost! Such sting
in mind make I. Path each for speed, 'tis true'
that differ not do they!' To mind these thoughts were new.

So now did stir a king as kissed awake
by birth in mind as thoughts seen not before.
Path hard made slow pace his. Each step did take
with care as light now dim, feet his unsure
of path. Alert as cry air pierced then tore
from mind thoughts his of path, rocks sharp and pain,
Saw he child young by path did sit and pour
tears large from eyes red hued. Ceased cries then feign,
to prince, not he upset. Face his showed prince disdain.

'Child poor, wept you so loud but why?' 'Got lost!'
Snapped child. 'From far or near from those who care
are you?' 'Nearby.' 'Yet lost? How came, at cost
of stress, tears large, that lost home near. 'Tis rare.'
'Know not do I. Light dims.' Lit fire to share
did prince. 'From where nearby do you then hail?'
'From hamlet small.' this child did point then stare
at distant fires. 'But lost said you?' 'But fail
might I the path to find! So lost!' at prince did rail.

Flow

'But you could I take there.' Too late this thought.
'And how, now dark, could you that do when I
in light, way know?' For child of hope, had thought,
when prince and steed were first espied. So cry
did cease but hope did fade fair swift and die
at choice of talk not deeds. 'But help need you,'
'Do I? Did cry when lost was I. To try
help give do you decide needs mine? Knew who
at time, when lost was I, needs mine so well and true?'

Then into night this child did slip then call.
'Time next, prince young, if help wish you to give
act swift in choice let talk be keen. To stall
in deeds for talk o'er needs of child forgive
not you can I.' As fire did stoke, pensive
this prince became as words him judged too well
from lips of child. Who helped could he if sieve
what seen when eve not dark but dim. Now fell
these thoughts like plates in stack as truth now rang like bell.

In distance far did seem way his through fire
must pass. So stumbled he through thoughts and dark
as fire now guide became. Thought he, 'Some pyre
must be, or stream from mount not seen.' So stark
thoughts his as choices none could take nor hark
to voice from past of choice to pass or make.
Now fear, not known in mind before, did mark
then rise in thoughts of prince. But think, not shake,
did he as spell of quest did weave to stand not break.

Flow

As nearer drew to source of flowing flame
its truth did dawn. Now truth of quest did grip
both heart and mind as sun did stir a name
and each did rise. The dark of night from whip
of fiery sun did flee. Then prince did grip
on hilt of sword as thought of beast who fire,
from deep below, on earth made flow which sip
do salamanders fierce. These flames seemed pyre
for corpse of quest for which would chant no choir.

Then stir awake to seek a bridge which strain
could take of fiery stream which fast did flow.
Now eyes and ears did seek, did seem in vain,
for sound of beast ne'er seen nor fought who woe
and death at man and steed with ease could throw.
With sword and shield for battle drawn and spear
untied for ease of strike at beast, 'this foe
unknown, unseen before, not I, on bier
will cast,' this prince now thought as beast did rise then leer.

This lizard beast then rose to strike as flames
did dance and swirl from tongue and claw then pause
as stone on steed was spied. This beast which maims,
no mercy shown, did drop its head and claws
of flame. Then nod to prince as stone whose laws
it sensed did call through work of dwarf. Then turn,
through eyes did show, that lead would it, by roars
of stream where flames with rage did roll and churn,
this prince and steed to place where flames could cross not burn.

Flow

This prince agreed, sword sheathed, then bow to beast
as meek, now he. That one so strong, no fear
of men or fight, with speed its foe released
did puzzle prince. Yet awe felt he so near
to one, though beast, of stone knew more. Ne'er hear
like such had he before. Of stone no thought
had he e'er giv'n. This dwarf, this quest, now clear
did know, this prince, that fate of more, was caught
in stone, than his alone. No doubt of quest now fought.

Was time not long e're beast did stop by stone
on which did twist and turn shapes strange. Here beast
and prince did part. By salamander shown,
was he ,through eyes and claws, to wait. Released
from call of stone this mighty one, great priest
of flame, did prince then thank, on knees, from heart
a greater one than he. As partings ceased
this salamander priest did clear impart
that wait not long would be then flew to flames like dart.

By stone, alone, as shapes did twist and weave.
Where beast was now in flames could he not see.
No bridge here stood nor ford to cross but leave
would he not do. The words to wait now he
obeyed as sun now high did burn. No tree
here stood for shelter cool from sun or flame.
No curse swore he at fate or heat. Agree
to wait had he. Through roar of flames their came
a sound of bell and oar. Could boat this river tame?

Flow

Through swirling smoke and flame came dragon prow
so fierce and high to stone on bank. Did grind
in bank, man strangely clad with oar, the bow.
Glance brief at steed then boat and flame as signed
to board was prince. So walk with steed to find,
in prow, a place advised was he. Then oar
in flowing flames was plunged. From bank there shined
light strange from stone which prow released. Then tore,
in flames and flow, this prow, by strength of oar to shore.

Flames' tongues did lick o'er prince and steed in air
so thick and sharp in throat and eye. But eyes
of ferryman unseen in mask did stare
at head of dragon prow whose eyes did prise
a path through scorching flame and flow whose cries
like winds around did howl. By prince unseen
on bank did glow old stone. Then he surprise
did show as boat on shore did grind then lean
So he could climb on bank not burnt and scarred but green.

Then mask remove did ferryman. Address
the prince did he for fee. With thanks was paid
the toll by prince who stared at flames' caress
now soft. As lean on oar a smile then played
on face of he who'd rowed. 'Young prince, if stayed
had you on distant shore to die not live
fate yours would be. Time first a choice now made
by you with balanced scale in mind. Did sieve
boat mine, need yours, flames harsh then self good judgement
give.'

Flow

'This river harsh no river is but sea.
This sea of flame 'tis wide. Seems this from shore
untrue as bank so close does seem to he
through smoke does peer.' Then thoughts, like mice did gnaw
on mind of prince. 'Time long since I through door
did step inside a castle dark. Inside
am I not out. In forest deep, light poor,
paths three, then one, took I. Say you sea wide
now crossed have I? Where now does wall of castle bide?'

'Before, behind, above, below, within.'
This ferryman did state as mask did place
o'er face and oar did raise. Unseen the grin,
by prince, in mask as prow, itself, did brace
for flame then shore release boat strange to face
flames bright. Did lines on rock flicker then fade.
Shapes strange on face of rock did seem to trace
this journey his. But mind and eyes no trade
could make so missed were these. Just tricks, thought he, eyes
played.

Pool stirred again by rod of dwarf to time
when four did leave and ride from pool. To west
did turn eyes his. Not smile did he, as crime
once done could yet succeed if fail in quest
did four. But face did set as stone as test
unfold in west did he now watch with eyes
bright sharp and mind so clear that doubt, no guest
at table his e'er sat and dined but dies
forbid to dine at table set for truth not lies.

Flow

Of brothers four this prince who west did ride
in heart was vicious cold. Aloof in deed
to those in need bar he. This quest had tried
to halt from start. In uncle sow a seed
of doubt tried he at brothers sneered   so need
of quest would pass. But uncle answered plain
that king would he not ever be if freed
by quest the king within was not. This bane
in place, till king return did he, would e'er remain

The kingdom feared rule his the most as word
always could trust. As plain words his when speak
did he. Lies none told he. Not one e'er heard
from lips of his. No mercy, love did leak
from he and none did e'er compassion seek.
His justice cold to kin and kingdom all
on needs of his rest did. So all deemed weak
by he if needs had they. No right to call
and plead that others share. Folks these did him appall.

Aloof heart cold rode he in forest dark.
Did yawn as int'rest none could he e'er raise
for quest as brothers rule would he. Not hark
to uncle's words as death would soon erase
the pointless need for quest perceived in haze
of uncle's mind. His father's dreams now cold
as stone where father lay. No honour plays
on mind of prince so cold to life. To fold
shroud cheap o'er uncle's corpse, plan his, thought he, not bold.

Flow

Not feel the forest rip or tear at cloak
did he. Then clearing he espied where three,
not one, clear paths did meet. Here sat, by oak,
man poor and old. In rags so thin sat he.
For bread in need was he. 'Man old, to me
now tell which way!?' Man old, did spit, then stare
at ground, with stick did play with leaves from tree.
Then pause and eyes did raise 'What way, to where?'
'To west, fool old, to west! Me tell or poor, by me you'll fare!'

This man did scratch and sigh then stand. Then lean
on tree and spat. 'No bread, not you, did share
to ease needs mine nor yours! Now prince so mean
with bread a plenty fresh, for me no care
does have nor I for him. Such fools, so rare,
like you on quests fail do and die. Answer
clear is. Paths three, choose one!' This prince did stare
at space then left where man did stand and slur
as disappear like prey so fast did wretchful cur.

But prince did shoulders shrug. No care, so choice
made he. This path through bog and marsh did lead.
But steed and he no fear did show. No voice
did hear as dry ground reached as fire did need
as sun did set and coolness feel. Now freed
from saddle graze did steed. Then prince did eat,
then sleep. Now moon so full did rise. On greed
of prince shone light of silver bright. Then meet
did light and armour bright by fire now cold in heat.

This silver bright did others see on plain
and light on ground at night was clue now sought
from tree of oak not far away. But strain
would ears to hear these move to prey. But caught
by steed on breeze, was scent. Some time this bought
this prince to wake, now stirred by steed, grabbed sword
did stand. But net did fall on prince, time short
awake was he to see. Blows fell like hoard
so sleep, unsought, then claimed their prey. Their laughter
roared.

As dawn and steed did call this prince awake
with sword and curse did slowly net break through.
So slow moved he as head and arms did ache
from blows. Now bread all gone cursed he those few
who wise must be for what did steal, they knew
like he, could ne'er be proved. so mount on steed
did he and leave. Now prince would none he view
as torn were robes and cloak. Blood his did feed
flies black. Swarmed they round neck and face and drank with
greed.

On rock ahead man old sat he. No grin
on face had he. 'Int'resting path to ride
at night chose you.' As crumbs did wipe from chin
did chide, 'If bread shared you instead of pride
a safer way would I to you provide.
But you, prince poor, must I now thank for bread
which others shared with me now warm inside
am I. Farewell fool poor on quest soon dead.
Soon fly and crow will come and feast on eyes in head.

Flow

  This prince did curse at old man's words. But burn
   in head did they so brief then leave and go
   like he that spoke not long ago. Then turn
   steed his to path. If learn, did he, not show
  in face nor mind did change. On flies or crow
  did he dwell not. Of quest e'en less was thought.
   For news of uncle's death desire did grow.
This dwarf and brothers three did waste time short
for life on quest but he, so wise, a queen he sought.

  Soon he a village small and coarse did find.
   Child small on wall did him survey. This pale
child poor and pale, with limbs so thin, seem'd mind
  this stranger's choice of road. From one so frail
  came looks so cold. Seem'd ice from eyes did flail
  the heart and mind in prince. Unmoved, alone
this child did stare through eyes of blue which veil
his mind and thoughts did they. Did feel like stone
so cold and dead that mother none would wish to own.

  Now prince so wary spoke in tones not known
   in he before. Though child's demeanour cold
did strike with spikes of ice through flesh to bone
now soft spoke he. 'Child young, help yours, if bold
   may I now be to ask. To west, 'tis told,
  where set does sun, can near to here be found
   a road. This way need I as man, so old,
  this way refused to tell for coarse the sound
of tone used I. For I in chains by quest am bound.'

Flow

Now voice of child was cold as eyes of blue
which stared at prince. 'Your bus'ness none of mine
this quest of yours. Care not do I if you
find west or not.' Like unseen thorn of vine
on flesh did words of child prick mind with sign
of poisoned barb in prince. 'Wish I that bread
had I to share and offer you so dine
with me might you.' 'Wish none, have I, so fed
by you . Care not do I if you alive or dead.'

Such words spoke he as eyes of prince held he
with his once more. The wall, and prince, then leave
did child, no look nor glance behind. Not free
did feel this prince from ice of child. But cleave
to mind these barbs of child and not reprieve
from these as child did part felt he. So cold
did air around become, for cloak now grieve,
did prince as sounds of drunken brawls him told
that small must he become as fear round him did fold.

Now cowed did he, with care inn passed. No sound
of he or steed did wish to rouse to fight
such men, with he, as brawled in inn. Then found
the child again did prince. 'Your help, this night,
could you have giv'n, to stranger lost, of sight
of road to west.' Off wall now climbed this child.
Eyes cold at prince did stare. No warmth did light
nor melt these eyes at plight of prince now mild.
But prince this look once saw before in beast untamed.

Flow

'Cruel, children learn to be can they.' shrugged child
as turned, no care for prince. Then left with eyes
and heart untouched. No wiles of prince beguiled
nor fooled child cold, too old, so young. Re'lise
did prince, lies none told child to he. Surprise
in eyes did show at meeting strange on road.
But west did call back he to task as cries
of crow heard he. So ride must he but bode
not well these cries from sky. Now quest seemed heavy load.

Now thunder rolled , so loud, through ground, not sky,
as river fierce did feel, not see. Such sound
of flood that quake did road and steed. Soon nigh
to angry river flow came he. 'Be drowned
will I if cross try I!' No bridge was found
as search in vain did prince. Then he a chain
did see on tree nearby was firmly bound
which crossed this torrent wide. Then crane
neck his and boat espied wherein a man was lain.

Now prince learned he tones new on quest and ways
that speech to strangers he, in need, must speak.
So now to ferryman asleep who lays
in boat at rest if help could he, so seek
the west might prince. 'Prince strange, polite but meek,
but yes can hire boat mine to cross for fee.'
'Fee yours have I not now since robbed by cheek
of bandits smart when I asleep so see
plight mine?' 'Oh plight see I, no fee, rest I, nigh tree.'

Flow

'Need I to cross with speed. Help none from you
then lost am I to fly and crow as feed
on me will they.' 'Words strange say you. Not few
words yours do my rest spoil so why? What need
have you that toil for wage, this fee, through deed
could pay in time?' 'With you must I agree
if time had I. This stone, now born by steed
of mine, for place where sun does rest, needs flee
from what not I do know, of quest am blind, can't see.'

This ferryman's eyes no clue of thoughts gave they.
'Fee mine, be paid it must by labour yours.
By hands of yours may river cross. The way
is clear, as agree with me did you, no pause,
that work would you but time had none. Though roars
the flow 'tis only way.' At this grow pale
did prince at sight of flow. Find now, from stores
within, must he, strength his for fee to sail
and pull on chain for distant bank to gain not fail.

To fee did prince agree and steed did board
then iron chain grabbed he. So cold this chain
at flesh did stab. But not, could he, afford
to yield to torrents stormy ire nor pain.
So close eyes his as arms and thighs did strain
to hold boat tossed to chain and fear did fight.
Seemed time too long in watery foe when gain
the bank did he. So stiff limbs his but plight
now o'er did seem on quest did shine at last some light.

Flow

But ferryman thought otherwise as boat
needs be returned. Once steed ashore, to chain,
did prince, find hand was fixed. To flow, this boat,
now forced hands his. 'My fee, paid I to gain
far shore. Not fair nor right that I more pain
must pay!' ''Tis fair that boat, to me, return
do you. For boat have you not paid. Complain
may you but hand remains on chain to burn
till fee for boat is paid. What agreed we don't spurn.'

So prince, twice more, did mighty torrent cross.
With ferryman agree did he that fee
to cross now paid. Unfair was he that loss
of boat, at first, could he, though prince, not see.
This prince did wave as boat returned to tree
where ferryman met he. Looked he to west
and quest through diff'rent eyes this prince. Now free
from dreams of news of uncle's death this quest
to him now called. A king within now stirred in breast.

In pool did rod now once more stir to north.
On face of dwarf, so still, was nought to read.
If troubled, pleased, on face not shown but forth
with final prince did eyes now ride. Succeed
these four, not fail, must they or lost the seed
of hope asleep in oaks where vigil held,
so still, for quest of dwarf. So great the need
of all in balance hung as fates did meld
the paths of all in one who dreamed this hope not felled.

Flow

This prince who north did ride a friendly man
was he and kind but cowardly inside.
Now cowardly and treachery these can,
and do, be seen, in one, through deeds. Abide,
through motive not, as one, do these. The guide
to those who judged this prince and deeds was fate
of those with him who rode. Lived some but died
or wounded others fared. To battle late
n'er he. Could fight but ran, as fear did open gate.

If one could lose this kingdom's throne 'twas he.
Unsafe did all in kingdom feel if rule
did he. Him ask to guard back theirs, agree,
e'en brothers three, nigh killed, 'twas thought of fool.
Shield his though strong for he alone, this tool
of war held he. Though deft with sword and spear
'twas rare for these to strike at foe, Not cruel
this prince but bound in life and heart to fear
for loss of self and life. But now to north did steer.

Alone in armour full rode he with axe
and sword so close to hand, but visor sight
on forest path made vague the way so lax
was he in haste. In time this helmet tight
remove did he as forest dark no light
could see through slit so small. Did ease the way
as eyes accustomed grew. No thought of flight
as yet did rise as fear did sleep, though day,
in night of armour strong and hand on hilt did stay.

Flow

In time did path in clearing end, but rest
this prince would not in place exposed where four
paths led. While coward he, no fool, this quest
to end in place where four on one could pour
from woods unseen with ease. If hear, not sure,
if crackle heard, alert stood he, sword free
from sheath. Man old, in clearing strolled. Was poor
was plain to prince, so bread not sword shared he.
Of path to north did ask man old now sat by tree.

'All three to north will lead but choose with care.
In one lies treachery so bold, that all
do suffer loss of time and hindrance there.'
'From where, which path, this fate will rise and maul
on way?' 'None knows when treachery will fall
from friend, from kin, from self. With care now choose
path to north.' This said did nod and call
'For bread, prince kind, thanks I you give but ruse
of fate know none 'cept life engaged and lived will bruise.'

'Advice to me like sand in hand which flows
and solid not to grip like water's drip
through fingers cold when cup is cracked. What shows
or gives no clue for me from talk? Now grip
mind mine a doubt but choose must I not slip
with quest exposed in clearing large. For why
and purpose what? Man old, did wish me trip?
With me did he not share, like bread, where I
might tread. With knowledge none be wise, path choose, to try.'

Flow

Alert now prince a path did choose. On plain,
grass green and lush did path emerge where trees
so ancient tall did shelter give. Dark stain
on green were shadows large, so cool, with breeze
which gently branches stirred. But visored sees
this prince not clear with shield and sword in hand.
This path no pleasure brought for fear did freeze
mind his, aloof was he to pleasant land.
Then crashed from horse to ground was he no chance to stand.

As helmet loose did he, man old in face
did loom as bread took he and left. No stare
at prince, no leer, no grin, no hint of grace
as knife withheld from throat. But bread, with care,
from steed, not gold, did take. Yet prince did share
with he. 'What treachery is this? did think
this prince as mount on steed once more. 'Is fair
this life to all like this to bruise? What link
deed this did bind to me? In me or he the chink?'

At side of trail did see man old by tree
in shade with bread. Then sword and anger rose
but thought of fall, though old, man this, strong he
to best a prince in armour clad, so chose
let anger stay unleashed. For fear then froze
hand his as helmet dented loosed. 'Betray
but why whom bread with you did share?' 'If knows
this not, prince young, do you, life's bruise this day
lost 'tis in pointless time. Show you, did I, the way.'

'Warn you did I that treachery around,
within, does lie. To best a prince not plan
of mine, whom bread did share. Thoughts yours, not sound,
like sand in hand are they. This plain, to man
and steed, so fair and kind to cross, where fan
does breeze from heat in day. Place this, so fair,
bread none does yield for men so old but can
if borne by steed. With visor down, no care
for plain, just fear, face yours unseen, bread yours did share.'

'If face saw I then pass would you through plain.
This treachery seek you in me. It lies
within, 'tis slave to fear's commands. Refrain
from blame of me. For treachery belies
a truth 'tis cowardice unseen which tries
its lies to hide. For fear of fear 'tis root
which deep within resides. To fear, 'tis wise
and useful tool in life. Protect, bear fruit,
can fear. But fear of fear bears canker deep in shoot.'

Before this prince could think to speak by tree
this thief of bread was gone. Did prince no ear,
for words of truth on bread, nor fear, have free.
These words could he match not to life. Sincere
was he the kindest prince of four. But cheer
mind his and spirit raise could not this thought.
For thoughts of bread and theft have nought with fear
to do so pondered he. 'Deeds mine have nought
which common thief can tell when bread stole he, not bought.'

Flow

But words had pierced somewhere in prince as now
no helmet worn. On edge of plain a girl
saw he, with hound, by tree. Life's weight on brow
did seem to prince so stop did he. Uncurl
did hound then teeth did bare at prince. 'No churl
am I yet hound thinks so?' Then girl did look
at prince and hound did stay by girl not hurl
with claws and teeth on neck of prince. 'Mistook,
did she, for brothers mean, who horses ride or crook.'

'Thought I when young a brother's role in life,
in part, was protect kin. Some lessons learn
did I so hound trained I my back, from knife,
to guard and kill or maim when one did turn
on me again.' As girl did speak, through fern
did creep then leap on prince these four, 'Oh No!'
These words too late for prince. First black, then churn
in head, did words, as struck a viscious blow
which felled from steed. How long lay cold not he did know.

When woke up he all gold was gone and head
did ache and stiff was he. 'Back mine not guard
did you nor hound?' 'Told I to you, misled
not you. Back mine alone guards she. Not hard
to see now why.' Then prince with thoughts now sparred
and fought as girl and hound no looks behind
did leave. Quest his by life felt burnt and charred.
As prince did rise and road survey was mind
then chilled as girl and hound did go where brothers lined.

Flow

This prince, on steed with shield and sword then fell
on these, full hard. These four, so well, did learn
of care which fights to pick. His axe knew well,
when swung, its game. On ground lay four whose turn
to fall now came. But two, whose blood, in fern
flowed free no day would e'er again see they.
As prince, gold his, bread theirs did take, was stern
that e'er sister theirs harmed again that day
would he return and slay this pair on ground that lay.

His point to make did scar cheeks theirs. Now hound
and girl emerged. Just nod did prince to her
as turned to leave. Then bread and gold on ground
in bag did toss and grin. Then point at cur
now cold in fern and two that lived then fur
of hound which hackled as groaned they. Then ride
to north this prince began as king did stir
within. But way to go was still inside
not known. from stream a call ,'To path will you I guide.'

In view, man old, then came. From blood,did clean,
in stream blade his. 'Perhaps, words mine to you
sense make? Those brothers four, hound fierce, did mean
to slay this day. Back hers took you and slew
as fit thought you. But one slew I. Hard through
back his this blade was thrust. For he so sly
in tree with spear did lie on branch in yew
unseen. Not four but five had she, not cry
will she that now has two. Thinks I that both soon die.'

'This road seek you to frozen north which ice
blades has to slice and gore and bears there live
who not do mercy know. Like tumbling dice
fate yours now stands. Me thinks that I, can give
a twist to load these dice. Then test and sieve
your fate will you. A brother mine the boat
does own on sea which cross must you. Forgive
life not this brother mine for north does dote
on him just cold. But he alone has tamed that moat.'

'For north a castle mighty seems which looms
with crystal light which eyes does burn if stare
too close or long. But this give I that dooms
this brother mine, with gold of yours, to share
from book of ancient past skill his. Will glare
fair fierce when token shown. Inside will grin
that token his returned, that thief did fare
not well when met by I and girl who pin
head his to stake did we, a point to make on sin.'

These two then wrists did take and part as friends.
To north rode prince where cold now pierced through skin.
But steed no fall on road did take though bends
sharp were at speed of pace its hooves vermin
did treat ice sharp which snow did hide.'Twas thin
this snow and treacherously sly. Then pace
did slow as blizzard swirled. On face no grin
though thoughts on dreams of warmth. Fought fears and face
did set this sea to seek, to end quest his did race.

Flow

This prince now far from where on ground lay two.
Groaned they and ached from fight as crawl each tries.
Then one did turn and point to tree of yew.
'Not two but three of us slain were. See lies
in tree no spear in sight and fear now flies
with pace inside that time alive is short
for us. For I no sword, nor blade make rise
to strike, protect, can I.' These two then fought
to stand or crawl. Knew they, from girl, no mercy bought.

Did reach the tree on trunk did lean when growl
from hound heard they. Then sister cold did say.
'This plain, a kingdom fair was once where howl
of wind and cold from north reached not. Here may
the trav'ler pay for skins of bear at bay
to keep the cold for journeys north, time past.
Such greed had you that not protect, that day,
as sworn to do, our king and queen, but cast
oaths yours in dirt, did you them slay. Take breath your last!'

'Not hound this work will do but I. This price
pay you as prince of mine in jealous rage
of me did first you slay. Then threw you dice
for deal of death to king and queen. Of age
am I too late for love now cold in cage
in ground there placed by you.' Now ice in eyes
did stare on two as spear in hand like page
of scroll did turn and weave in breeze. Then flies
with force of loss and rage her grief she satisfies.'

Flow

These two on trunk spear pinned as one now dead
were left as food for fly and crow. 'Deed done
as planned with unexpected aid,' Now said
man old as comfort girl did he. 'To run
as wolves did they on prey, did duties shun.
For king and queen, love yours, can we not raise
from grave. But kingdom can restore which none
will e'er gainsay on plain where once did graze
herds ours and corn once grown for bread which all did praise.'

Of this did prince no knowledge have as sea
was reached at last. At sight of floating ice
mountains eyes his in wonder stared. No glee
did him though fill, as boat, to he, suffice
would not this sea to cross. Then he advice
old man did give recalled and token gave
to ferryman. Glared he, as warned, with vice
like grip at prince. Then shrugged and grinned did wave
this prince on boat with steed. No oar in hand but stave.

'My back take you for curse of ice at boat
is thrown. This kingdom cold it welcomes none
till sea is crossed and valour shown. This moat
a crystal sea can be as tricksy spun
was curse till ancient book through wit, was won,
by me.' In waters cold was thrust this stave
which rang and sang as ice it struck. Not done
with pain this prince, once more, did stand, now brave
with axe and shield for battle raised as back to save.

Flow

In leather armour boatsman clad, the cold
seemed not to feel. But soon words his came true.
As ice did break and scream its shards did mould,
then flew, as spears. Then shield and axe did hew
and whirl, no rest, could prince now have as few
the times when air was clear. Then boat did beach
on shore of ice and air still fell. Then view
did prince their journey made. 'A sea? But reach
place this in castle ground? Of this books none do teach.'

This ferryman did grin and gold return
to prince. 'That gold take I in case repair
this suit have I to do. As few do learn,
in crossing fierce so short to fend from air
where spears do come so fast and thick to tear
this jerkin strong. Not torn, no need for gold
have I.' Then wave did he, then sit, no care
for journey back a while but rest from cold
and wonder how this quest of prince would now unfold.

Now rod in pool did stir once more as all
now needs be seen. On face of dwarf, so still,
did nothing show as stare in pool. Then call
did he in tones too low for men. But fill
the pool and air these tones did seem instill
commands to winds, these tones, to carry far.
Then tones did cease and pool did churn as skill
of dwarf with rod now brought, old man with scar
from mouth to ear, to watch all four like fish in jar.

Flow

In time a place by each was reached where steed
would suffer much. So reins and saddles worn
and bag with stone remove did they then freed
these horses four, with thanks, to roam. All sworn
to see their quest fulfilled with stone now borne
on back did seek a way unknown by they.
But now the kings within awake like dawn
began to rise. Paused each in thought. To stray
from path not known if true best stop, rest take and stay.

In east, the prince, on land so high, of breath
was short. In distance mountain loomed in sky
did seem the stars to reach. To climb was death
knew he so trust and wait plan his to try.
Unseen an eagle far did prince espie
and dive then mighty talons strong did bear.
to mountain's crown and place this prince on high.
Then prince did feel at end of world on stair
to moon and stars as night now slept in stellar glare.

In south, air thick, now furnace seemed. Did burn
and scorch the way. Great stag, for prince, now came
to bear both he and stone. Soon heat did churn
and seethe as stag did seem to pause. As frame
a thought, did prince, a lion stood, not tame
with mane of golds and browns. To prince was clear
as respect paid by bow to these, no shame
felt he that lion strong, had come by here
to give the strength that he had not, so felt no fear

Flow

As ev'ning fell and air did cool did feel
that edge of world drew nigh. Then eagle flew
this prince to mountain top which once did deal
to land and air ash grey and molten stew
of rock and stone. But slept, now spent, prince knew
by coolness underfoot. Then moon did show
to north the land but void in south no view
but stars and night. As warmth did die did grow
now cool as prince did wait for what did he not know.

As prince to west with stone now walked was sound
of foaming waves which lashed so hard a shore
which soon did come in view. Then pool was found
which oddly still in storm did feel. As roar
of wave did crash in wailing wind prince saw
a salmon rise so huge 'twould dwarf a ship.
On salmon's back did he then step. It bore
to west through oceans, seas where time did slip
then slide. Then mountain rose like glass, seemed moon did
clip.

Then eagle dived and swept this prince to where
did feel a star could he now touch. Seemed space
and time beyond this place did cease to share
their meaning clear with he. Then stone did place
by side and watch a silver moonbeam trace
a path through mount of crystal clear to east.
'Tis odd to feel alone but not and brace
mind mine for what not I do know. But least
of all do I now feel yet warmed my coldness ceased.'

Flow

In north the cold, thought he, could bite no more.
But wrong thoughts his did find. This bitter air
spikes gave in every breath to lungs. 'Not sure',
thought he, 'if rest or walk will death now bear
to me in shortest time.' As this declare
did he did ground begin to shake then claw
of bear did raise and place this prince where share
its warmth could he. Wild lands were these prince saw
but bear alone was left , too feared, claw his and roar.

This prince through blizzard wild a change perceived
as ground did rise. This bear in dark cavern
so dark did go As prince did bow, retrieved
stone his, sound strange did fill the air. Then turn
to see dark stairs did rise and torches burn,
'but lit by whom?' did think. 'Sounds strange, like loom?'
Did ponder brief as stairs climbed he to learn
fate his and stone's. Did feel, on stairs, like tomb
left he, so still, the cave. "Tis life face I or doom.'

Then summit reached as stairs so steep did end.
To north was nothing seen. No land, nor star,
nor moon did seem to penetrate but fend
off light did this strange night as black as tar.
To south could land of frost and snow so far
be clearly seen as lit by moon so full
which seemed so close. 'To reach and touch would mar
this jew'll of silver near,' this prince did mull
over in mind. 'In sleep, dreams mine, would now seem dull'.

Flow

In dark of night in pool did dwarf now cast
old ir'n rod his like spear. Then two did stand
to chant old songs began as both, in past,
together had when more there were who hand
in hand would chant and stand . Each prince in land
so far away did rise as stir did air.
From far below in earth did stars command
bright towers five of light to rise and pair
with towers five from stars and merge as one for stair.

Then princes watched a mighty one descend
as stones, from dwarf, did rise, then crack and flare.
In east a sword so great did truth defend.
In south did staff of justice rise so fair.
In west rose graal of love outpoured with care.
In north rose shield protection give and guard.
At mighty ones with signs returned did stare
these princes four. Then sleep did fall so hard
as quest its toll did take. No sleep, this sight e'er marred.

As princes slept these mighty four in light
of tow'r o'er pool of life . These signs then placed
'twixt earth and stars in tow'r which shined so bright.
Then chant of dwarf and friend did change in haste
undo then seal the work of thieves now raced.
Thiev'ry undone and sealed, to dwarf returned
rod his from pool. Then sit did they and faced
once more pool dark and watched as water churned
to see these four return in whom kings four now burned.

Flow

As each on mountain top did wake could see
in lands a change. Descend did they in sight
of day, bar he, in north. Who stairway he
in darkness night's to cave, choice none, as light
of torch did lead that way, did take afright
as woman stood eyes black, hair black, robe green
and point did she to veil of stars in night
from whence did sound of loom arise. Now seen
on loom was life of princes four, now kings, foreseen.

From mountain top return did these to steeds
not gone but stayed to wait. Transformed were these
from colours five to four of old. Now needs
of quest undone by uncle kingdom's keys
free giv'n would be. But now, for test, which sees,
if kings or princes flawed did ride or not.
If sit, would they, on thrones, now fate would tease
from four truth clear by deed, instilled, begot
learnt not, for king to land is bound by sacred knot.

Did dwarf grin now to friend, ' 'tis time so rare
to know if thievery undone now stand?
As only king oath theirs break can, if care,
in blood which runs, through bond, to sacred land.'
For now, pool round, did mist of grey demand
that dwarf give way so they four kings could greet.
This dwarf did nod, agree, now thieves, to hand
so close and grin. ' For four, now kings, defeat
can we through simple talk to cause from oath retreat.'

Flow

    Now wait for they in mist who walk no fear
      friend old nor dwarf did show but sit, not pray,
and wait. Then dwarf, friend his, through grin, did steer
      to cards, on which did figures move, to play.
      As wait, did all, with ear and mind on day
    which end did mean that truth, or not, be gained.
      Mist grey did form begin to take as they,
whose work, which dwarf and thief undid, had stained
with blood and treachery a land o'er which none reigned.

    To pool did four from journeys come and sense
      that test of quest now came though tired and worn.
    Saw they that dwarf and friend, in cards for pence
were locked, then grinned. 'Friends grey, to east once borne
      by quest was I. In pool a truth stillborn
      does lie.' 'In south, did I, a balance see
    in pool so deep.' 'In west, of love, forlorn
    does chalice weep.' 'Friends grey, in north's cold sea
did see what pool last took. So look, kings four, bid thee.'

    Then folk of grey did laugh, 'Oh dwarf and kings.
      see oath is dead, now free in pool to look,
    unweave, are we now bid by kings whose rings
      of oath to dust will fade and scribes in book
      will write of foolish hopes of those by brook
      in temple oak to trust in dwarf and quest
of men.' So northern prince, now king, then took
    ir'n rod of dwarf. Did bid folk grey, not rest,
in mist as solid form in pool to look was best.

Flow

Now people grey round pool did stand and peer
as king ir'n rod on pool did float with care .
'Pool dark, as kings to land now bound, appear
to these do we command what last did glare
that took did you so deep to depths. Now share
with these so eager seek to see.' Then shook
the ground and oaks around as stirred in air
change strange. Now pool did swirl as what it took
to surface rose and king did bid folks grey to look.

Too late for them form mist to take as stone
their feet became then legs. As eyes too late
did recognise the eye of one alone
which pool did take. Now bas'lisks death and fate
was shared by those whom kings and dwarf berate
with sneers not long before had done. Last sight
of these was dwarf with rod. Ears heard, as state
fate theirs, words last from dwarf, as stone last light
of mind and thought did crush from life this cursed grey blight.

Then six did stand, some time, in parting's grip
till kings and steeds past lions strolled to way
which path to kingdom lead. On road no slip
made they and uncle's face did show that day
that dwarf word his had kept. Word his betray
would not to king so now stepped he aside
so four could rule. In kingdom all did say
of these kings four as years did pass that bide
in them did father's heart and mind so strong inside.

Now rode from brook and oak did those to meet
with dwarf and friend by pool where statues grey
like guardians stood. As chants did rise and greet
days new for hopes and dreams once more to play
in minds of all. Then part did these but say
did they,' another's quest begins when moon
is full time ninth from now. Far not away
from here in Ahma's womb will rise quite soon
a candle flame so bright not born of man but tune.'

At this did dwarf and friend old grin as stare
in pool now still. 'Months nine to rest and play
friend mine, at cards for pence and song then share
once more our journey long till Ahma lay
on sheet of white and child of tune greets day.
Then quest shall rise till tasks ten his fulfilled
through journeys hard, for him, no easy way
will be as tune needs then a player skilled.
For now, rest we, by shadows grey and cool till filled.'

Flow

Prelude

When first did I through Hafren's kingdom roam
through forest tall and false by river wide,
did seek path steep to Hafren's head on loam
fair damp. Track climbed did I till stand by side
of pool so small from whom do torrents ride
and flood. Then she in robe of green did stand
with hair of golden hues. In eyes did bide
greens deep with browns. 'Know you name mine?' As hand
did raise asked she, 'or why stand you on sacred land?'

' 'Tis easy known by I,' low'red eyes, reply
gave I. 'For Sabrina name yours. For sing
do nymph and sprite of you. Songs theirs did fly,
in times long gone, from here to kiss the ring
of apples gold on Summer's shore to bring
touch yours to Avalon. 'Said well,' spoke she
'for Saisen young.' But disappear on wing
unseen did she when answer next on tongue rising.

From Hafren's head did journey long to hill
by waters bound and steep which Ambrose stole
for fort nigh Gelert's resting place. 'Twas still
as tread did I when druid's dove, on knowl,
feathers so black, by grove did call, in role
of guide. Through orange beak did me command
to hoary man. Drew he in leaves nigh hole
now filled. 'Know you name mine?' As hand
did raise asked he, 'or why stand you on sacred land?'

Flow

' 'Tis easy question asked,' bowed I as state,
'Merlin name yours and father none had you.
Hole filled, so legends say, did harbour fate
of land and kings. As white and red then flew,
and battled, wrestled they in night that grew
that man and king be wise yet fools became.
Once mad, thrice dead in one, fate yours. ' 'Tis true
what Saisen young to I did speak.' 'Then flame
unseen hid he and answer cease of land and name.

'Twas afternoon when lake reached I to rest
when dream of snake so white did rise and fall
as call from sage to pupil rose in test
of change. Then wake did I to face a tall
Lady in robe and hair of black like pall
did feel as eyes of night did order stand.
Now tremble much did I and fear the call
of voice to come. 'Know you name mine?' As hand
did raise asked she, 'or why stand you on sacred land?'

' 'Tis easy question asked,' bowed I as shook
and stutt'ring spoke. ' For Ceridwen whom seed
through winter bears when Brighid's work from stook
is done, are you. Corn blue, also, to feed
folk faye in hills that dwell, guard you. But deed,
which mem'ry holds so clear, is birth of child
of radiant brow who sailed in skins, once freed,
from anger yours to Elfin's shore.' Not mild
tone hers o'er I did weave in wind unseen and wild.

Flow

'Tis truth young Saisen child. Words old spoke you
of times when I and men did cross in life.'
Then gone in wind was she. Then lake took hue
by I unseen before as castle white, like knife,
did carve a path and rise as panic rife
did tear through I. For rode a knight on wave.
A mighty steed so white did bear through strife
with lake this knight in silver mail and pave
a path for shore. Thought I, ' Is't here, meet I the grave?'

Then steed did halt as sword unsheathed did point
at throat , 'Know you, Saisen, name mine?' As hand
on hilt did tighten stern. Then shapes adjoint
on blade did move and weave an eerie band
nigh crystal edge. Bare speak could I nor stand
with ease, ' 'tis easy question asked of me.
As Mabon you then known. For lost from land,
taken were you 'twixt bed and wall e're three
days old till Arthur's knights did seek, did find, did free.'

"Now Saisen tell to me, 'as sword at ground
did point then rise once more to throat of mine,
'this land neath feet of yours why sacred found
to all?' 'Tis easy question asked, for line
of time unrolls to when from west did sign
arise. Invaders harsh did come to wage
wars theirs for land through death. To east, like swine,
were people herded, pushed. Did anger rage
at loss of life. Sought these lands new in which to age.'

Flow

'As people fled did stories keep in mind
and heart till land of forests deep and green
by mountains borne in mists so grey did find.
'Twas place where stories hid and grew unseen
from west till time in books were scribed. Could lean
on staff at last these hoary bards in peace.
For red and white and black made these serene
then feel as task, from journey hard, release
them did as burden passed to page and toil did cease.'

Then sword to sheath returned as golden child
now knight did bow and grin. 'So Saisen friend
know you what lies in stories old?' Now mild
in tone did ask. ''Tis easy words but end
do they in riddle deep which mind attend
to must. In stories old is all and naught.'
At this did mighty Mabon roar and send
to trees a laugh so loud did flocks who fought
and bickered flee. But I, relieved, felt life I'd bought.

As farewells bid did knight to castle ride
cross waves. In time did sink, was gone and air
did seem strange clear. So now no time to bide
by lake did homeward weary tread. No care
for questions more but one this day so rare.
As I did home nigh reach neath slates of grey
where welcome glow from doorway called. To share
some chat did enter in as voice did say
and fav'rite question ask, ' which ale want you this day!'

Flow

Origins

1

Rose Aquila from cave in void where high
on wall, in nook, did eyrie rest and cling,
in light so dark, 'twas hid in shadowed sky.
Then called to cranes, did she, their patterns bring
to weave around the spheres of night which sing
unheard and chant of time when all was still
in naught. For her, with mind so clear sorting
what eyes so sharp espied, shared she, with skill,
with cranes. These patterns scribed then cranes and skies did fill.

2

For now were stars in ferment wild. As fire
and molten rock did dance with steamy air
in motion born of thought then light. Attire
this naught of dark with light did breath so rare.
From chaos ordered thought did rise and flare
then fade to midwife's chant, 'in breathe, out breathe,
now rest. In breathe, out breathe, now rest.' No care
for fear of chaos, blood and water's flow which seethe
then break as cry breaks forth. This chant does she then sheathe.

3

Aquila soared with cranes through dark and skies.
Record did she and they, of what, in time
in mist, would fade unknown, unseen in lies
from eyes which upward squint and peer to climb
and grasp, believing equals are, though slime
born all from dust of stars, to sacred breath. But she
and cranes this knowledge seen ignored to prime
this firmament of awe and wonder free
to share through patterns clear to eyes which wish to see.

Flow

4

To eyrie she returned for rest to wait.
Now time, begun, relentless sand did hour
by hour pass through its glass. No fate abate
this ox whose plough not stop for rest in cosmic shower.
But count, where number's start unfound, this plougher
its furrows tamed in spirals, twists. Then mark
it left of path in stars. But knew no bower
for rest would be as time and number hark
to none to cease so onward marched celestial clerk.

5

Aquila flew when ox ten thousand thousands
spirals ploughed. For certainty alone was change
which she and cranes did store, record, as hands
unseen turned glass as ox did mark the range
of ordered time and space and naught derange
this ox from task e'er could. These spirals traced
did cranes. For Aquila's sharp eyes these strange
patterns ordered in mind, revealed and placed,
by her, so spiral maze became in crane encased.

6

These flights made they as aeons passed unseen
by none but they, this ox, and mind from whom
this ordered chaos brought through melody,
whose weft and warp did weave a chord on loom
which ox, and she with cranes, then traced this neume.
From wings of she, for crane to scribe on wind
of stars and spheres, this chord and neumes did she exhume
from ferments fierce which rose and fell. Rescind,
bestow this neume, could they, o'er time most disciplined.

(Neume is plainsong chant. Derange to throw into confusion)

Flow

7

As melody and time did weave and leave
mark theirs in universe expanding fast
did ox and she keep pace. Here change did cleave
then bond these stars and spheres like clouds now cast
with dews and rains of light, then dark, like rainbows passed
did they unseen in aeons old. As time
relentless ploughed unyoked symposiast
with tune, new laws, unsaid, which bind and chime
through loom this rain to dew and light to dark this cyme.

8

For now to Aquila's sharp eye and mind,
as once more she and cranes did changes map,
that spiral furrows ox did leave revealed that bind,
did melody and time through law, and trap
these clouds of stars and spheres. By numbers strap
with cords unseen so bound had they become.
Still move did these in ordered way with gap
where play did flotsam still unbound by thrum
and drum from loom whose chord, unseen, a hand did strum.

9

On these did word, millennias past once breathed, echo,
demand it done, 'Be Light !' First cry from Light
outside of time now Aquila mapped. Foreknow
not she nor crane as she from source from night
to light was called to be to fly with sight,
a gift received in void from shadowed sky.
Now she and cranes did trace once more a bright
new dance in ox's maze of lights where eye
could see and trace new pulse arise where stars did lie.

(*Symposiast: One who attends a symposium.*
Cyme: The collective flower of a plant which which has a single flower which develops first then from here develops through higher orders.

Flow

10

For laws now bound to melody, motion and time
did separate for some so day and night
were born. Here ox gave birth to ox, so rhyme
and harmonise these spirals small and tight
to beat of time would furrowed be. This sight
of Aquila's sharp eye to cranes relayed
so flow from naught to all, so clear, would write
on cycle's, spirals small as tune which played
by unseen hand. The tune since time began ne'er strayed.

11

To rhythm beat begun so long ago
and slow, infil now born did frantic seem,
yet even 'twas in spheres, which spun, though small, still slow.
As beats in beat did set the pace of stream
of finite time which flowed in law's regime
from melody and time,' in breathe, out breathe,
now rest,' did midwife's chant from ancient dream
arise. For then did all and naught bequeath
on gold the day and silver night to chaos sheathe.

12

One sphere did still in chaos seem though day
and night now born. As furnace roared within
its molten surface steamed but sulph'rous clay
did alter, change, as clouds so thick not thin
obscured the heat of day. To cool did clay begin
in silver light of night so cold which bound
by clouds when day remained did form a skin
so clay and water part did they. Surround
and flow through clay when water depths and cracks it found.

13

Flow

As clouds dispelled and poison ceased on sphere
now cycles new emerged complex yet small
Aquila called to void. From cave, like spear,
black crow through time and space then flew to call
to map these cycles small. Through hunger fall
from task did crow. Meat red and dead desire
did crow and thoughts became confused, unclear so shawl
of ignorance cycles did cloak in mire.
Now crow's desires unbound brought death as burnt in fire.

14

Once more to eyrie Aquila did turn .
From eyrie perched in void did raven black now fly.
Observe and map did raven black. Not spurn,
at first, this work for map, not classify
nor specify did raven black. But eye
did see for cranes to scribe. But soon did mind
distracted grow as filled with awe. Then sigh
at task as tired did rest, meat red to find.
Now raven's mind unbound brought death as flames confined.

15

No despair rose in mind of she once more
then call did she. From depths of cave now flew
a bird with stars in feathered tail. Did soar
and glide through space and time with ease. Its plume imbue
with colours rich of purples, gold, and blue
did stars. This peacock roy'l did strut, not play
as take up role with eye this world to view.
In lake did see unknown beauty on bank did stay.
Now peacocks sight unbound brought death as burnt that day.

16

Now called from eyrie flew a bird so white
and pure. Majestic she, endowed with grace
now flew on mighty wing in day's twilight.
Then she to task began to bond as trace
in air, on land this wondrous place
so cranes could scribe. Soon she did find an open sea.
Now map under and o'er did she, embrace
this task too close, exhausted fell, had she
no mind for self so saltwater tomb hers would be .

17
Now flew from eyrie crystal light as dove
did answer call. Now he could sense in soul and see
the tiniest spirals weaved complex by love
and thought in spirit hid which ox, ne'er free
from plough, had traced. So dove began to empty
mind his of all that seen. Too complex were,
too quick relayed for cranes to scribe as he
grew lost in what was sensed. No use for task as stir
did soul unbound so he in fire did death inter.

18
Aquila's task nigh done did she summon
a bird, now rare e'en where her eyrie lay.
A phoenix came at her command from sun
and rest in void. The phoenix flew each day
and night, helped she, to cranes, this bird relay
all patterns started long ago. Then air
did change as age of creature came to stay.
Aquila flew to cave in void. Cranes stare
as phoenix old did burn to ash in fiery glare.

Flow

Ahma's Labyrinthine Child

1

Now dwarf did glance at friend, stones grey then sky,
'To dust must folk grey crumble now for their
forms cold are best not found by curious eye.
But first, to know the who that they, once fair
before to mist did join, did breathe this air.
For one and eighty round dark pool now stand.'
Then rod at nine did point. 'As dust now share
the fate of beast and lie unknown on land.'
From dust did rise the shades of those in life once grand.

2

'That merchant old, when young, knew I,' spoke friend
to dwarf. 'Now we do know these folks of grey
which warnings heed did not, in past, so end
as promised, fell on them by pool this day.
For he so sharp in markets far away
did catch the greedy eyes of kingdoms nine.
Then each a fleet did give and gold to pay,
to bribe, negotiate dream their's. So all, a line
did cross. Forget did they as soul did fade and pine.'

3

'...More grieved am I by second shade now seen
for he and I would fish in streams when young.
Till he, when father died, on plough did lean,
complain. 'To dream of ours, o'er time we've clung
so plough o'er life not loom as weight. Hard flung
this plough by whim of fate which dream from me does drain.
This early father's death of dream makes dung.
So I to plough, to sow for endless grain
am bound. Alone, must you, seek those, mind yours, to train.'

Flow

4

'Dream was to nurture soul and balance toil
with sense. But fear did he, at early loss
of father's light then gain of farm, that soil
would other's wish to take. So choice of not to cross
river unknown made he. Life his did toss,
e'n wife and child, to kingdoms nine for gold.
In time saw dream of ours as childish dross
told he to me. Wife his did leave and told
was I that son, eyes blue, now walks with heart ice cold.'

5

On shade of kings' commander both did look.
For he in life ill famed and foul by all was seen.
Though armies great all suffered much that took
gold his to serve and fight, e'en die. At scene
of battles his, oft more of these on green
of grass did die than enemies they'd fought
and beat. For all, to him, were pawns unclean,
a sacrifice for naught these warriors bought.
A cold mind his, yet warm for gold was he in thought.

6

' 'Twas he who thief so skilled did find and pay
to steal from hall of oaks the four which sleep
in quiet pool this day. But he, on day
when bargain kept, thief slew. Gold his to keep
now silent thief in blood did lay, as cheap
to him were lives to spend.' Did dwarf relate.
'From four, untouched by hand till then, unseen, did seep
a mist so fine with song within. So fate
from fools, in time, through song, unwound life theirs' once great.'

7

'These six who fade, not six, but legion were
in life. For these did arts pursue for gold
and fame not beauty's gift to move and stir
up heart or mind. This first of six soul sold
to nine for furnace fed by mount of fire now cold.
No artifex of purity were these
which ore did melt and craft for tools to scold
both land and men so nine, who ruled, would please.
Not feel, did they, at what craft their's unleashed, unease.'

8

On rod did eyes of dwarf then dwell and sigh.
'For these did cast with craft, from gods once torn,
in moulds so rulers nine could play a lullaby
so men and minds to sleep could put. So torn
were men away from dreams, all knowledge shorn
of land and nymph, signs four. These gold did mint
to coin to prove the rule of men as pawn
to self alone was knowledge true. Not stint,
did these, in furnace fierce, where sweat, like gold, did glint.'

9

'Songs sang and chants did these which now do wilt and fade.
Were sirens cold, in kingdoms nine, to those
who fought nine kingdoms' rule in mind. Betrayed
by songs so gently breathed which soothed then rose
as fog in mind. So thoughts 'gainst nine then froze
with dreams in tomb.' Then dwarf to friend did turn.
'Songs theirs did lengthen task of mine. Oppose,
unseen, search mine for signs did these. Though churn
songs their's, betrayed did they what I did seek to learn.'

(Artifex: Alchemical term for refiner of metals)

10

'Betray gift their's, of song and chant did these whose voice
did lift to honour greed and praise of men.
Now songs so silent cease to stir as choice
made they for flesh, not heart, nor soul back then.'
At dust did dwarf and friend now stare as wren
did skim and stir with wing as dipped close by.
Then point did dwarf at shade of sixth. 'Impen
skill their's of tune did these from muse so lie
could they to self and all, through note and chord, hereby.'

11

'For these did tunes for singers' songs create.
As masters played on pipe and four stringed lyre.
The trump of war used they to stir for death, berate
foes theirs so kingdoms nine through blood and fire
and pain more land and people gain. No byre
for peace would ever give. This beat of drum
relentless throbbed as hearts for war ne'er tire.
In temples built to honour men did some
of these the stolen chord on lyres of gold once strum.'

12

At this did friend of dwarf now nod as stare
at dust in thought. 'These three whose shades now fade,
the last of nine, did carve, and build a stair
so princes nine in clouds could stand. If stayed
hands their's had been when warnings fell, alive, not shade
would each now be. Then painter cold did catch
this sight on temple walls as proof now made
of man as god. E'en city gates did match
this scene. Twas then that plan to steal the four did hatch.'

(Impen: Enclose)

13

Now dwarf to pool did turn with rod in hand
which stirred to sight these kingdoms far away.
The walls and gates of nine now fell. Not stand
did they, but crumbling were as rod held sway
o'er those, now dust, these walls who'd raised. So grey
the air as temples fell. No glory now
as pictures ground to dust by pestle stone and clay.
Then mighty gates did crack and groan as bow
to weight of crumbling stone as keystones crushed like plough.

14

Now snapped from dreams did people wake and flee.
Some fill hands theirs with gold and silks did try. Like sand
these two through fingers fell as dust. So see
could they as veil like blindfold fell as hand
unseen did loose. These kingdoms nine on land,
as waste, now fell. No stone on stone did stay
uncrushed which once by artisan made stand
as miracle with craft and skill but lay
as sand no glory now, cornerstones theirs just clay.

15

In harbours deep and grand where lights at night
did ships guide safe now sea and wave did claim.
Fleets nine did creak and groan as wood did fight
with metal bands as rust consumed and nails did maime
planks theirs with rot and bile. These ships of fame
now lame with mast and oar as shards, which sea
did take to sleep on ocean bed, now tame.
Cargoes of jew'lls, soft silks and gold now free
did sink, decay, thought dwarf, as waste of stone and tree.

16

As cities, kingdoms, harbours fell a cloud
of dust did rise to hide the sun and light.
Now spread this dust to field and crop once proud
of corn of golden ear. For fearsome plight
of starving hunger harsh did rise in night
of day, so bleak. So flee did those from fields and plough
once slaved by siren's songs which once did blight
thought clear. But dust to lung, throat dry and brow
did cling and choke. Fell they on dust like broken bough.

17

At innocence so trapped as slave, now dead
in fields and towns, did silent dwarf and friend
low chants begin and draw, in place of dread,
these souls now lost by Styx's edge and end
confusion's plight with bridge of light. To spend
too long by river's bank seeps form from soul
till clear and wraith becomes. Chant theirs descend,
so swift, to rivers edge so soft did weave and roll.
Now silence fell o'er kingdoms nine where death the toll.

18

As clouds of grey did settle, fall, then hail
did stir this dust with clay as corn of gold
and grass of green crushed lay as wind did flail
clay grey with mingled tears and blood, now cold,
with green and gold. E'en crow e'er bold
refused this feast of death. So time and rain
a grave would dig and bones to earth return.
'Now sleeps moon first of Ahma's time. 'Tis lain
in dark of sun to rise,' sighed friend,'not yet her pain.'

19

By pool in light of dawn did dwarf now turn
to seventy and two, which cold as clay
now stood. Then rod at nine did point, return
this stone to dust and mist of shade. 'Betray
men all did these of minds so sharp. Did play
with words as toys and bribes to bend the ear.
Music and arts' philosophers which stay
the soul were these, the worst scientia, steer
kings nine to meas'ring all so rule, as truth, was seer.'

20

'For these, cool minded, sought to measure soul.
No scale, nor rule, nor bath could prove its place
in men. E'en gods, with nymphs and sprites,
like soul saw they as childish dross. No trace
of these could prove. So sought did these to race,
create, advise so thrones to man on stair
in clouds was placed. Then those of arts embrace
did they these measured ways,' friend grinned as dust by air
was spun then dropped. 'So Styx's flow will much them scare.'

21

Now dwarf, at eighteen forms did point with rod.
Now these so brittle were that shades were pale
just clear enough to see. For they no prod,
in life, of conscience felt. For these did rail
at prince and slave in temples cold and stale
with incense bought with blood. Priestesses, priests of rule
were these who all did bind through oath and fear. Impale
on spikes would they Like hen,
were these then caged, to pick in mud pearls false in pen.

22

Tired dwarf and friend did watch these shades now fade
and meld with morning mist brooding o'er pool
and reed. 'How cold in heart was plied their trades
as artificers kingdoms laid so thief as fool
could hide the four at cost of lives. Like tool
once used these tossed the lives of slaves to death
in seas, in mounts of fire. 'Enough! Like stool
from rear of death these kingdoms nine! Not Teth
this kind can stand nor take to heart for mercy's breath!'

23

So dwarf at these, who dead and cold did stand,
did summon rod to bring to dust and clay these last
and turn away from shades who lives on land
did leave to rot as build stair theirs. Now passed
the shades of kings, all nine and queens in past
with advisors so cold in hand and mind.
As seers tossed flawed and false made dice. Once cast
these weighted were by numbers known which kined
fate theirs in patterns known so future safe defined.

24

To pool did dwarf then turn once more and stir.
Dismay at sight not show did he nor friend.
'Stair theirs remains when all is dust, concur,
doubt none, do we friend old to chant the end
of stair is work for Ahma's child. So tend
must we so paths revealed where choice is key.'
Now dwarf and friend did rest with cards and question send
to those in hall of oak by brook, as free
from quest awhile these two, if steps next did agree.

(Teth: See notes. Kined: speared by prong of pitchfork or fork .)

25

So far from pool where dust and flesh now lay
did sorrows nine arise to weep o'er game
of kingdoms nine and all who slept on clay.
As they did travel land of tears no name
found they for those this pain so vast invoked but shame
at minds so cold for self and glory's sake.
For here lay child unborn. Barely the flame
of life touched they in womb, no water's break
did these e'er see, nor face of she who helped them make.

26

On children lost did sorrows pause and weep.
For these too young for work did run and play
in fields and streets their games. Some close near home did keep
to mother's call, too young to play and stray.
For these no future call now could. No day
when trade of father, mother they might learn
would come. Did sorrows weep for these who lay
by friend or mother's side. But these not turn
from fate e'er could, as choice removed, in fire did burn.

27

As kingdoms travelled sorrows nine so groaned, so wept
at sight of youth who'd life begun to live
and learn. Here some who lay first touch had swept
through heart so passioned love and lust did give
fervour unknown before first primitive
and fumbling, clumsy brush of flesh and joy
of kiss. Such waste of young initiative,
hands theirs and minds once deft and keen, employ
would not for future work. Nor love would these enjoy.

28

Roaming these forlorn kingdoms sorrows wept once more
for those just wed or soon to be who lay
apart in dust so cold and grey. Death tore
all future dreams of child, grandchild away.
Here rich nor poor fared best nor worst this day
but now as equals lay both slave and free
ignored by crow and fly. Could these not pray
for mercy's hand to stay this fate, nor plea
of innocence nor guilt for kingdoms' infamy?

29

Here too did lie, for sorrows' tears to kiss,
all those for whom, now children gone, more light
was life to bear and skills now honed did hand not miss
what steady eye did see. Did life seem bright
till dice did fall and four touched were in night
when all did sleep and trust. Did fall dismay
on kingdoms' dream as mist could they not fight
nor halt when four were sealed in pool that day.
So sorrows wept for innocents king's deeds did slay.

30

These sorrows nine did lament loud and wail
at price of greed in kings. For those once fair
in hair now grey did lay too soon. Not frail
were these who knew some ease from life and care.
No autumn days for they to show how young could bear
with pride this life of toil and joy so short.
For earned had these through life and work a share
of lighter load. For these were they who taught
how tool or child be held but by dust grey were caught.

31

Then sorrows nine with softened tears did weep
for those of hoary head of gentle grave
now robbed. Sat these at village gates where keep
age's wisdom, not for self, as free or slave
advice could seek. For these, twixt two, could pave
a way peaceful through strife, but these now lie
neath crumbled walls now dust. For gates protect nor save
could they from fate as drawn by those in high
temple or palace grand. 'Such waste,' did sorrows sigh.

32

As sorrows grief, at cost of kingdoms nine
intent, did ebb and flow till change arose in tune,
of songs and chants, as turned to where malign
fell curse on creature, land and plant. Though soon
would these recover first, tears warm bestrewn
like silver pearls did fall on land and sea.
Then chant did change for final time as lune
round kingdoms nine did form through melody
of tears and chants as these did cease their eulogy.

33

This grief outpoured did ripple pool which friend
and dwarf did watch so far away as change
foreseen in cards so strange began. 'To end
so much too soon by deeds of mine, thoughts mine derange
would sorrows seen. Chose kingdoms nine to range
too wide and far and warnings heeded not.
Untouched by fate of people theirs, exchange
minds theirs for stone or ice did these in plot
to wrest from pool the four where failure fell as lot.'

(Lune: Enclose in sphere by ascending and descending arcs.)

Flow

34*
'Be cured of mist if pool had left alone
had they, all those now dead alive would they
now be. But all they ruled, land theirs, did own,
with foolish kings all fates were locked that day.
For king and land were one.' Did dwarf sad say
with sigh so deep to friend. 'To take on kings unknown,
unwise the grey folk were with fate to play.
Then those who ill advised as fools were shown.
For king from north, in trust, rod used as stature grown.'

35
Now friend and dwarf, in setting sun, did muse
in vigil still. In silent thought did their
minds cease from louring thoughts of fate. Then hues
of reds and golds did blend like fiery air
'mongst clouds of silver, white. Sight this so fair
did ease and calm like autumn's hints of rest
in winter days to come. At sight so rare
did dwarf and friend release, for time, thoughts theirs' of quest
to come as sun did kiss leaves green of far forest.

36
As dark of moon did rule and blacken night
did friends observe a diamond sky till fire
did sparks release like would be stars now bright.
Now passed had Ahma's second moon soon tire
would she in labyrinth deep as child in byre
of womb did stir and grow. Slept she for now
as pace kept she, news none did she require
of dwarf, nor friend so dreams arose. Neath bough
in hall of oak did bard with harp all dreams now plough.

(* This verse refers to the events at the end of Book 1)

Flow

37
Aquila rose from slumber long in cave
in void where shadows danced and played like trance
on walls and mind. Did call to bird in trave
of cosmos born to glide and watch the dance
that Ahma's child would lightly tread and prance.
Bird grey from north to south and back would fly
and watch and note. Should any kill with lance
or spear or arrow fleet in trave would die
where bird so slain did fall. These were Aquila's eye.

38
For Ahma's child in womb did call and ask
such questions clear and bold of life and death
and stair of men on mount, in heart. Not bask
in womb so warm and safe this child but breath
did seek to see, and find, what severeth
when life does cease and bird of grey does note
in mind so vast, and dwarf's meaning of Teth.
As seven moons did feel too short to grasp by rote
this knowledge sought as tune of bard round babe did float.

39
In dreams of dwarf did message rise so clear
from hall of oak by brook on notes of tune
from hands of bard. In dawn's first ray appear
o'er pool did cranes. So dwarf and friend attune
did they minds theirs. For trials round journey strewn,
knew they, would rise. 'Time not for us through gate to ride.
to Ahma's child but seek we first, as moon
does pass, the market place, near rising tide,
where thousand faceless strangers' silken tents abide.'

(Trave: A cross beam of restraint)

Flow

40

For dwarf and friend, knew now, from west did three
for hall in oak now ride. In dreams had friend
and dwarf often these met. For one was he
of radiant brow of stars.'Twas he did message send
to hoary friend in windowed tow'r, descend
should he and leave a while. as one that stands
where choirs do never cease and chants n'er end
now walked, in darkest light unseen, o'er lands
for council called neath oaks, with egg, star specked, in hands.

41

This bard that wove in night did sing of crane
which died when melody in womb did spark light bright
to life. This ancient crane by death was lain
where ash of phoenix yet, unborn, from sight
of all was hid. Somewhere knights four in night
of tricksy keep now slept. Here child of gold,
with wisdoms six, in cave 'neath keep of light
on lyre did play and sing to guard this hold
of knowledge rare where quintessence does flare, unfold.

42

This dwarf and friend full knew this keep did call
which hid like lovers do when hide and seek
play they. So help did need or fail and fall
would quest now set. So cards did lay but weak
the thread twixt they and keep but hope did peek
enough for dwarf in pool with rod to stare.
Now thread did path become then maze. Neither did speak
as pool searched they for clue obscure to where
path vague to maze began but pool seemed not this share.

43

Then dwarf song low did chant o'er rod and eyes
did raise to clouded sky. In ear a cry
in distance heard as she, once gift, now flies
to friends by pool to perch on rod held high.
This hawk did sense what dwarf could not. Once more did'st fly
so far from pool to peek and pry, its prey
to seek ,which hid, or seemed, from pool's clear eye.
So dwarf and friend did sit once more to play
at cards for pence till sun, on hills did seem to lay.

44

In sunset's reds and yellows bold, did cry
from sky alert these two of hawk's return.
On arm outstretched of dwarf did perch as morsel dry
was giv'n. 'At dawn's light first leave we to learn
what rod did show to hawk,' spoke Dwarf as turn
to friend once more with grin. 'Seems time and life
do richly weave new tales to spin yet yearn
do I for time when journeys cease. Yet fife
now calls to march,' grinned friend then spat and wiped old knife.

45

These two did ride from pool in dusky morning grey.
Once fed, off rod did hawk then rise and soar.
'To west of north go we where veil, some say,
'twixt dead and living, vague becomes. Unsure
become the minds of men that fear this lore.
'Tis time long gone since tricksy place did tread,'
did friend relate. 'but recall I that four
unseen, unknown held are in awe. Now dead,
doubts none, is she this told to me as trade for bread.'

Flow

46

' 'Tis strange,' did dwarf reply, 'in mem'ry deep does stir
a journey made by father mine but pale
in mind now age this clouds but when closer,
perhaps, recall will I.' Then storm of hail
and rain unleashed by angered clouds did flail
at face and steed. Did gallop hard to wood
nearby but mercy none from wind, with wail
of she who forebodes death, was shown to hood
nor oak. Did torrent flow where once old town had stood.

47

This fierce storm uprooted, tossed like hay
oaks old and sleeping ash. 'No shelter here
safe is for us!' Did friend to dwarf then cry, 'But stay
nearby must we as storm does path unclear
now make and seeks distract eyes ours through fear
of flailing oak and flood. But trust the cry
of hawk must we for she, eyes ours, like spear
does cut through storm! But soon a change sense I!'
But raging winds seemed words to jeer and judge as lie.

*48

Like dragon prow to boatman blind did hawk
become to friend and dwarf, now soaked to skin.
Both bones and steed did ache from storm. Did stalk
and probe then pry in mind to tricksy win
this wind. So lost would be if not for hawk through din
which cried with eyes bright clear. Then storm gave way
as heat and sand became land strange. Did grin
these two as rest awhile as steam did play
and rise from clothes and steeds. But change again sensed they.

(* Reference from previous book)

49

For sand did wreathing serpents seem so eyes
did close as lead steeds their's where hawk's cries clear
did urge. If eye did glimpse then tricksy lies
would stumble cause to serpent's coils then dear
the cost to trav'ller lost was death through fear.
For sand, unseen, firm was neath hoof and boot.
In time sand firm now drifting dunes became which steer
the step astray and hawk did try to mute.
This shifting dune unseen did hamper all pursuit.

50

O'er time did dune give way to meadow green
where grass, in breeze, did rise and fall as ocean wave
on wave on path as shore. Here rest serene
did seem though brief as hawk did call. Then gave
a glance, did dwarf to friend, with grin, 'Like slave
feel I of fate times oft.' Then mount did they
to ride once more when night, though day, like grave
did fall. 'Not tricksy night,' did friend then say,
'But land where veil is thin. Walk we with care this day.'

51

'Are close now we to path in rod to maze.
Heed not the calls of those long gone nor nigh
that walk these grasslands dark. Eyes ours not raise
from path must we. Respect, to these, this shows. This I
did learn at cost,' sighed friend to dwarf. So eye
to path was fixed and ear closed to those
who news did seek of those once known which lie
this day in arms of life. Here breeze that blows
nigh cold or hot seems still, yet not, moon none e'er rose.

52

Did seem eternity did hold these two
in grip like vice. Some voices known in air
did rise then fall then rise again to woo
from path to idly talk once more and share
jokes old and woes. 'Respond, the veil could tear
'twixt death and life,' did friend in solemn tone then note.
Slow went on path in moonless night, as care
of step did take, sensed now change new as coat
of night did slowly lift and sun on them did dote.

53

'Twas strange this place of day and night as see
these both could they so clear. But journey's toil
it's toll did take so rest for time by tree
which marked this border strange. This yew in soil
of light and dark did stand. Round trunk did coil
green ivy old and gnarled. No voices crept
from either land past guardians these. Trefoil
abundant here did flourish white and red and slept
'neath boughs of yew. Now steeds did graze as hawk watch kept.

54

As passed moon third did dwarf and friend reflect
and muse on journeys old in moonless night
where clouds obscured stars bright. Somewhere there pecked
beak sharp on bark till hunter's claw did smite
and silence drew from night. Now fire light
did flicker, roar to bring moon third to close.
No cards for pence did play as sleep did fight
with mind, tho' tired, to force welcome repose
and rise of dreams as bard once more old song then chose.

55

In womb did Ahma's child unborn now turn
and toss in sleep then stir. 'In dream was I,
to thigh, in river slow, seek I to learn,
of sage who next to I did float and lie
in robe and beard of white, closed mouth and eye,
yet speak did he, as arms crossed were on breast.'
To find 'I' your's plunge me, must you, not try
but do, neath flowing river slow.' 'As test
did feel which obeyed I and gave to sage death's rest.'

56

'Quick eyes then turned, at splash, as one did race
so fast at me ploughing a furrow wide.
Then sage did speak,' 'this one must you now face
and wrestle close 'neath flow to rise inside
as one.' 'Did barely words these end when tied
was I in arms so strong and she in mine
as into river plunged. Like fish hard tried,
then bird, then wolf and lizard green then whirled like line
did pull to stand, of she and sage sight none nor sign?'

57

As question asked was heard in hall of oak
were dwarf and friend on tricksy path to maze
while steeds did rest by ancient yew, 'as yoke
to ox does path, so strange, now seem which plays
with eye and mind like curious child. In haze
of thoughts obscured by mist. Does path walk I
and you or we walk it?' 'Long not, this phase,'
did friend reply, 'for path is guardian nigh
to maze and key to gate unseen in wall by eye.'

58

'If tricksy path finds not a motive pure
then maze ne'er seen will be.' For dwarf and friend
on two paths walked not one. 'Alone and sure
must each walk path. 'Tis said oft times, of friends, came end
when two here walked. Did one, a fool, pretend
to motive good so path did dissipate,
ne'er more did these e'er meet again. Not wend
nor bend does path. 'Tis bridge of twine which weight
of fools will snap, then into chasm plunge as fate.'

59

'..And reason why in pool unseen by I,'
did dwarf reply. To dwarf and friend did path appear
to foot, as eyes firm closed, in wood to lie.
But each did walk a crystal thread so clear
o'er chasm black and deep, if seen strikes fear
if motives dark as maze appears for eyes
then open must for final step. But here
did dwarf now grin to friend as gate now lies
ahead to maze and final step of no surprise.

60

'At centre friend meet we. For sense, once more,
do I that each alone must sleepers find,'
grinned friend to dwarf. As forward each, so sure
did step, alone became in maze unkind.
For all did change and move and throb, unwind
twixt solid, liquid, air and flame. Did rest
now dwarf in centre's dome as friend appeared. Here shined
no light nor darkness black yet here, no test
seemed clear so rod on floor did place for clue to quest.

61

Then over rod did form bright crystal sphere
of constant change of pulse and dancing mist
and flame. This shattered loud as di'mond tear
did form and dome did open wide. Now kissed
by rays of many coloured lights did gold become, persist
did rays till rod did rise then rest as dome
did close and dwarf did rod retrieve from *cist
of light so old. Then maze did whirl and roam
till friend and dwarf in cave of night did stand on loam.

62

'Not knights did I expect like four just met,'
grinned friend as harmonies did rise and call
from lyre to wake in sleep and dream. Then sleep as net
did fall. In dream did golden child to hall
of oak now sing as wisdoms six like wall
of flame did dance and chant round sleeping friends.
When dwarf and friend awoke were they neath tall
yew old by steeds. In mind song soft, which fends
off doubt, did sing. 'Know knowledge sought child golden lends.'

63

Then singing faded soft under moon bright as day.
Did friend and dwarf now rest till bodies' needs
recovered were. Then passed once more by way
of forest strange of night in day which leads
through wild and changing lands to pool. Here steeds
did drink till cool as rod in water placed
once more. When rod withdrawn and raised did beads
of water drip on pool and forest traced
round ancient mount. Did whistle dwarf at what was faced.

(*Pronounced Kist)

Flow

64

So hawk did soar and search for prey of quest and way
to forest old. Not till nights four had passed
did she return to arm of dwarf, fifth day,
to morsel red and fresh. Then she, repast
full done, did fly, seemed cry, 'to quest at last,
begin do we.' 'To east of south flies she
where giants once free roamed. Their nets did cast
so dragons catch, could they, for steeds mighty
to ride. Their cities great now lie as dead debris.'

65

'Tis told,' did friend reply, 'of forest old
round ancient mount. Did I believe just tale
for fireside nights twixt warriors and kings, where bold
plans theirs prepared for battle fierce. Regale
with stirring tale would they so brave, not frail,
would sword and hand on field of blood next day
be wielded true. In forest dark ne'er fail
did quest some beast to slay, like foe, to lay.
But tale ne'er told beast's name nor who had claimed to slay.'

66

The southern sun seemed smile as air did warm
o'er misty lake espied through distant haze.
' 'Twas there that we first Bas'lisk met in storm
of hail and gale,' grinned dwarf, 'but now path strays
to east and desert warm. 'Tis odd? This desert plays
as swamp of cloying damp then back to sand
and heat. Seems changing path now acts like maze
unwalled.' As swamp once more became let stand
warm steeds from swamp to drink, though hooves in desert land.

67

'Now which to forest leads?' Did friend wonder,
'is swamp or sand the path?' Then hawk did cry
and warning give that something came. Thunder
did seem as hooves of beasts at speed did fly
cross land. Then mountain rose and forest high
and old engulf them did as ground around did quake.
'This forest lives, is beast of tales, sense I,'
grinned friend to dwarf. These trees did stretch and shake
as if awoken were. A silence did these make.

68

'Look now for slope and break twig none must we
and safe, think I, will we then be,' did dwarf, as stare
at path. in whisper state. From ev'ry tree
hung lanterns strange of rainbow hues so rare
which constant changed so path, not here, seemed there.
'Twas slow, pace theirs, till slope at last did gain.
Did rest neath dripping boughs. Like fetid air
of swamp did feel 'mongst moss so dark whose stain
each bough and trunk did wear. 'Tis time to walk again.'

69

This both agreed as drips broke silent peace
when dwarf and friend did fall through path to naught.
For now in mount both dwarf and friend did cease
in time to be, to think or conscious be as caught
were they in mind of one where time nor thought
held sway. Then she from void did urgent fly.
Cry hers did open scar on mount which brought
these two to rest in sun on summit high.
Unseen was she by two that slept 'neath starry sky.

70

Though moon was pale its light did wake these two.
    'Feel I dissembled was,' spoke stirring friend.
  'E'en though light's dim,' smiled dwarf, 'do see a clue
      by mound of ash yet warm lies journey's end.'
  For crane there lay so still in death. 'Seems friend
        that phoenix red keeps pace with Ahma's child
    for ash is warm.' These two did chant as tend
and place this ancient crane in shroud. When wild
a boar had been but now, as shroud, was gentle mild.

71

When crane in shroud safe placed then sleep uncalled
    did fall as mount and forest old did fade
  till phoenix rise again. Their dreams not mauled
    did dwarf and friend awake. By dew arrayed
were they by desert morn nigh swamp where played
    a horde of dancing, weaving flies round steeds.
  On steed was placed with care shroud full as laid
with chants for journey long. Then dwarf, on foot, steed leads
as he and friend do stroll while hawk on lizard feeds.

72

'Now west go we to land of rising tide
  friend mine,' did dwarf now note. As sun did sky
    traverse, to shady grove did briefly ride
  these two by sharing steed. As sparks did fly
    from welcome fire these two in silence pry
through thoughts and dreams for something lost by mind
    in mount. 'How then came we to wake nearby
where crane and phoenix lay?' were thoughts that lined
both minds till slept. In dreams did they no answer find.

Flow

73

'As float do I in waters warm do dreams
of mother's flow o'er me as she in breathes
out breathes in constant sleep. These dreams in streams
do rise and fall to beat of drum. Bequeaths
to me, this ancient drum, no rest but seethes
unceasing soft with music far away
and strange, it weaves in colours soft and wreathes
around in waters warm where stars seem play.
There's something lost know I, but what or when, which way?'

74

'For words do I recall nigh bridge long crossed
in time that drink was I forbid to take.
But why can I no answer find as lost
in mother's sleep and dreams. Like child on lake
of purple light sleeps who in who? To break
these waters now, too soon sense I so clear.'
Did child in womb now muse as sense not make
of dreams and mem'ries old. For child unborn, not seer,
in womb did float in colours, sounds, symbols unclear.

75

'Twas journey long to quiet pool where rain
stain washed, from bank, the last of statues grey.
Then dwarf and friend cart hitched to steed and rein.
With care did they shroud old with crane then lay.
So each did armour leather don. Then spark and play
did blades on spinning grinding stone. So small
knives these, like needles sharp, in hands did lay.
For time to journey south nigh west did call
from market far away. Shroud's fate could none now stall.

76

A song, so soft, did dwarf sing clear in ear
of steed with cart as mount did he and friend
on horses fresh. For twelve long days did steer
path theirs to west till trail to south nigh west did bend.
As cold days four and nights too warm did end
this trail nigh gorge of blackened earth and rock.
'Not friends nor foes are those whom gorge defend
far land of rising tide. Seek they to shock
and scare mind ours so round will turn whilst they us mock.'

77

Did friend now wryly note and eyebrows raise.
Then steed with cart, from leading rein by dwarf unhitched
was onward urged, unhindered on till haze
obscured from sight. Then tiny blades, when pitched,
as sparks from bellowed furnace white bewitched,
did blaze and fly, as dwarf and friend them threw,
at gorge of blackened earth. These blades then itched
earth burnt awake till gorge as titan grew
and eyes through clouds did dwarf and friend now coldly view.

78

Then dwarf and friend, steeds theirs, did urge to speed
through tunnel formed as tow'ring titan glared.
This tunnel cold 'neath gorge did steeply lead
to river dark and flowing slow. Bright flared
a light and walls revealed. No rock space shared
on walls for eyes this tunnel lined. These past
and present read in dwarf and friend who forward stared
with progress slow like river's flow. Not cast
did they eyes theirs around in light and tunnel vast.

79

Did feel eternity this scrutiny
which probed and picked through hist'ries past and weighed
'gainst future's likely paths. Then time did flee
and movement cease. Here light and shadow played
with mind and soul as cavern reached. This place now stayed
these knowing eyes. Lake dark this river slow
did feed where lights of gold did glow then fade.
By pool like dark abyss did dwarf then show
rod his and in pool place so guardian he would know.

80

As rod retrieved did friend and dwarf become
two crystals golden bright. In lake could see
dark merfolk graceful take and weave this light. Here some
did sing and chant. These songs so strange many
never would hear. From song and melody
of golden light last breath, for final fight,
for strength, the dying take. In breathe slowly
then out this gift from golden crystal light
before they briefly rest for time in death's dark night.

81

Once golden light so freely giv'n and freely shared
did dwarf and friend as selves then stand in awe
so long. At silv'ry light these two now stared
which ship, no sail nor oar, did guide to shore
where unseen hands with ropes, and weights did moor.
Then loading planks in silence low'red so friend
and dwarf, with steeds, could board. Both saw
cart bare with steed. Then message one did send
unheard and slowly ship did turn for voy'ge's end.

82

'O'er cheek can feel breeze warmer flow from quay, where we
soon stand,' soft spoke dwarf tired to friend, 'and crane
from cart seek we in market place. Nigh tree
in constant bloom of blossom red now lain
is she and so for Ahma's child remain
does she.' Did feel so long till light of day
in distance seeped and quay would ship soon gain.
As closer drew did sounds of bustle flay
all silence still from mind. By quay did ship soon lay.

83

So disembark and force way slow through mass
of faceless strangers they did go. To all
that sought to recognise did so in vain. For pass
like ships in night do these unknown. No call
could hear but flow of stars and tides which fall
and rise and recognition none need these.
Eyes theirs which tunnel lined did see through shawl
of secrets hid and trav'llers needs. No fees
or price in market place e'er paid nor need to please.

84

'Ride we through desert harsh till market place
reach we, 'called dwarf to friend in rising heat
and swirling wind which sand did flail as mace
through air on armour leather worn. Did beat
like drum of unrelenting march. No thief nor cheat
nor fool could e'er this desert harsh survive.
Here dunes did rise and fall like waves. Deceit,
these shifting, rolling, seething dunes seemed drive.
But friends ride would till they in market place arrive.

85

Here desert eased as cooler breeze did flow
o'er dwarf and friend. Here sand and dune gave way
to grasses rich where unknown flow'rs bestow
alluring scents. As far as eye could stray
were silken tents. On these did sunlight play
as rippled were by breeze. But silent awe
did fall on dwarf and friend. Eyes theirs did stare and stay
as wall of tow'ring, em'rald ocean saw.
Did seem frozen in time and space not bound by law.

86

'Did hear of this in stories old and doubt,
did I, t'were true,' low whispered dwarf, amazed, to friend.
'Tree ours does yonder stand,' did friend point out
as nod did he to dwarf. This tree did bend
and sway. Its blossoms red as blood did send
on breeze a perfume wild and strong which rose
petals and spice did bring to mind. Now end
of journey long drew nigh now tent's repose
by tree made clear as scent, on dwarf and friend, bestows.

87

Through open flap did enter in where light
of silk made all seem gold. Inside did stand
a tall and faceless stranger silent white
in robes of light with new sewn shroud from cart in hand.
Not speak but thoughts in minds did share, expand
on cloak for sleeping Ahma's child to wear.
'In cloak of crane inscribed is time unplanned
since Aquila's flight long from void to where
and when did spark of tune appear in womb so rare.'

88

'Child hers in womb from cloak will learn of all
that was before first spark and cloak will grow
with age. Then birds of grey, from trave will call,
send cloak, sight theirs. For child, will grow and know
that one did die that cloak be made. None show
this cloak till three that wait by brook in hall of oak
are reached.' Then stranger shroud from hands let go
to those of dwarf and silence bade so spoke
did none as stranger's form did fade as light did cloak.

89

Then scent of tree did call from tent friends these
where steeds and cart did wait. Here then began
their journey far to hall of oak. To ease
path theirs was trail, not hard, revealed which ran
to mouth of blackened gorge. Now friend did scan
and search earth green for hidden trail once known
through places lonely lost to most. A plan
had they, for contact none desire had strongly grown
as moon soon fades. Soon path to dwarf by friend was shown.

90

Through ruined castles old and towns long dead
did these two pass in peace unseen, unheard.
Here ghosts of ghosts did lurk and drift unfed
so long since body walked and breathed. No bird
here sang of dawn's day new. Feathered nor furred
passed not by here where moss and tree did rule.
'Tis welcome lonely silence this that stirred
and stilled the mind,' did friend now grin, 'and cool
is air. So fire make I for night by yonder pool.'

91

'In moons times four will breathe first breath as break
these waters warm will I. Did dream of place
where all was dust and dust was all for sake
of what? Light none, sight none had I to trace
in dust name mine. Here archive felt like case
of dreams unborn, unused by trav'ller scared
of motion to or fro till death them face
and case remains with dreams still packed. If cared,
for life and priv'lege seen o'er fear, would better fared.'

92

'Did see through eyes, mine not, a river flow
so dark to sea 'neath cave. From whence does spring
or source now lie? Oh mother mine does know
but not reveal to me in womb warming
and safe does she. But songs to me does sing
asleep which weave in mind and blood of place
that I face must when born and down it bring.'
So dreamed the child awake in Ahma's womb. 'But trace
will I this river back to source of two that race.'

93

By silent pool did dwarf and friend now rise
for journey on. 'Remember now do I
the stories gone of trail ride we. Once eyes
did see the glories here in dust which lie,'
sighed friend as each on steed did mount and try
ignore aches theirs that ground so hard and cold, as bed,
did freely give in sleep. As time passed by
through walls and dust trail old through forest led.
From lofty branches strong hung castle gates o'er head.

94

Tired rusted gates did creak in wind gone now
was need and purpose theirs. E'en cornerstones
and keystones too did trees enfold. Endow
did moss, stones these, a gloss of fading whites. Like bones
or trophies won did seem now high on thrones
of boughs, now kings of all were ancient trees.
But silence deep and cold did seep which owns
this place which reluctantly shared with these
old trees and weather sprites whom nothing sought to please.

95

'Twas broad and long this barren land now crossed
by dwarf and friend who revelled in its nothingness
of endless peace and calm. Too tired this lost
forgotten place to care of two which press
and carved turf green with hoof and wheel. Caress
nor pain this land now gave where once would test
each quest of all. E'en ghosts of ghosts not dress
the nights with fearful wails but idly rest
and float and dream of naught, e'en death, with empty zest.

96

' 'Tis worse than this in world of men fear I.
For kingdoms theirs do quickly rise and fall
to rise again then dust become,' as eye
did scan this plain of towns long gone, did call
and sigh, to dwarf, friend old, 'But soon this shawl
which barren land does cast must lift as we
new path soon take. Not long ride ours from there to hall
of oak and journeys end,' did grin to see
on face of dwarf relief then smile, 'of quest nigh free!'

Flow

97

In ear of steed with cart did dwarf now sing
and rein release once more and both did rest
as armour check and blades, so fine, did ring
as strop caressed and honed. 'Little int'rest
have I in fights and battles now but strength invest
will I once more and foe undo,' then swore
did dwarf to friend with eyes of ice. 'To best
foes these will us press hard. Fought these before
have we and won at cost but after this, no more!'

98

In distance they dust watched arise and race,
did seem, way theirs. So dwarf did whistle low
and steed with cart did bolt and gallop hard with pace
for hall of oak. 'Tis changeling folk, not slow
were these to learn of cloak,' as grin did flow
to grimace fierce, noted did dwarf as point
rod his at ground where mist did rise as blow
to sight so close must fight. 'This mist disjoint
mind theirs from eye in change 'tis then let blades anoint.'

99

As changeling horde did mist espy 'twas then did see
in distance steed and cart. Ordered were two,
which hawks became, to retrieve steed and free
cart old of prize which they now claimed, from who
did hide in mist, as theirs to keep. Into
strange mist with care did horde slowly then go
to seek, then strike with glee their prey and hew
like beasts untamed. 'Does press,' thought dwarf, 'this foe
so slipp'ry nigh,' as floored by unseen heavy blow.

(Strop: Leather used for sharpening razors)

100

For bear, o'er dwarf, now loomed claws raised and set to kill
as dwarf did roll as blow then fell and tore
and slashed at armour strong and flesh until
did start to change and blade of friend at claw
did fly, from wrist did sever bleeding paw.
Then dwarf did strike the killing blow as change
did fail. Peace none as wolf did leap then soar
in change to hawk but blade, as mist derange
its eyes from mind, did strike and slay this changeling strange.

101

Each time did slay or wound, friends these, did seek
to closer roll to fringe of mist and steed.
Then dwarf did pause as sense a change nearby where creak
heard he so then dispelled rod's mist so freed
to see were all. As mist did clear not cede
defeat would changeling lord, but cautious, thought
of those sent he for cart. Though done, this deed,
of them no sight and dwarf and friend, not fraught
with fear did him concern. Hand raised so respite bought.

102

On cart was shroud untouched and steed did graze,
raise head, then graze. As mist from ground did fade
were corpses six revealed in twisted phase
of change so beasts from dreams did seem. 'A trade,'
thought lord till met dwarf's eyes of ice, that coldly flayed
this thought from mind. Then dwarf on cart did place
hand his with shrug. 'If trick, by dwarf, is played
then slay, no mercy giv'n! And leave no trace!'
Then Lord and three did change till dwarf did humans face.

103

These three to cart did move, blocked not, path theirs
by dwarf. As each on shroud hands placed did peel
as thread became . In horror watched strange pairs
of hands, once theirs, appear on shroud. Appeal
for mercy not could they. These three by heel
were grabbed by friends, they too, as thread became.
As lord did seek to change did blade him find and steal
voice his as three as corpses fell from aim
of blades. Then all did watch as shroud all six did claim.

104

Now changeling foes unsure did stand and stare
at fallen lord whom speech had none and those in shroud
who now did count as eight. As dwarf, no care
for these, friend bade on steed to mount. As bowed
to lord did blade release from throat, 'Not cowed
by you were we. Mercy? None begged? To you
none giv'n,' as blade was thrust through heart. Not proud
foes these, now nervous, looked at lord as knew
did they what dwarf and friend who played with blades would
do.

105

Then sky was filled with ravens black and horde
now frightened knelt transfixed as one did dive
then stand in human form nigh fallen lord.
'Seems I indebted am once more. Fool this did thrive
by breaking law of changeling gift. Alive
would I preferred but dead do I accept.'
Then raven cloud, at sign, on horde did dive
and eyes did pluck. 'No sight need worms. Have kept
word mine to lord now dead,' snarled king as to friends stepped.

106

Then wrists, this king, did bond with dwarf and friend
and in cart peered. ' 'Tis work from market place
sense I from tent by tree that blossoms, end
ne'er do, of red and only fools deface,
like these, would try. Thanks mine, give I, but trace
one more must we so take leave ours.' Did nod then wave
at parting king both dwarf and friend. Unbrace
did they now armour warm and wounds did lave.
On steeds did mount last glance at field of worms then gave.

107

Path soon did ease so time took they to rest
and journey slow in time of fading moon
till final day remained of trail and quest
'twixt they and hall. As sun did set was soon
night dark then held by fire at bay. Then tune
from friends did rise as played at cards for pence.
Then sleep did they as dreams revealed a hewn
and regal ancient stone which sang of when immense
was thrust as mountain high through earth in turbulence.

108

Then some did come with craft. These pain did deal
as into stair did turn. From hall of oak
did harmony of bard this lament heal
and soothe as hope did share and light invoke
for peace in sleep. Here ancestors then spoke
of life in death and death in life then death
in death and life in life which sleep did stoke
so peace on mind could fall like holy breath
out breathed, in breathed at steady pace for strength of Teth.

Flow

109

In dawn's grey light did dwarf and friend now rise
with aching limbs from ground in night and fight
with changeling foes. Wounds theirs did smart, surprise
nor wince did show as water cool seemed bite
on flesh not soothe. For time did walk so light
on steed would final day of quest then seem.
'Two moons have we to rest by hall till sight
of Ahma's lab'rinth calls to us through dream,'
calm stated dwarf as point did friend at gleaming stream.

110

Stream bright, did both friends know full well, to hall
in oaks would lead. So mount did they to ride
once steeds refreshed by water cool. Recall
did they this journey theirs as side by side
did slowly ride till welcome sight that hide,
from prying eyes, the path to hall did see.
For spring, did seem, from crack in rock to bide
neath oak long dead. As rod then raised came change as tree
revived and grew and arch create as dark entry.

111

Once through arch dark did tree then wither, die.
In distance loomed tall hall of oaks where stand
did council calm. Dismount did friends. Defy
their pain did they. Then steeds led were by hand
of stable men to brook with stall and land
of fertile green. Then dwarf, quest's prize with care did place
on stone in council hall. 'Now we command
let healers tend wounds yours with herbs and lace.
Then feast will we so strength have you to council face.'

112

'For story yours and friend's some time will take,'
so smiled sharp eyed old man in robe of white.
So dwarf and friend with healers left. Did make,
these healers wise, friends two to sit in place where light
was bright. Then balms prepared to soothe. 'Some fight
had you see I, but changeling folk?' 'Gift's law
broke these at cost of life,' did friend with spite
in voice relate. Then wounds, once dressed, did draw
blades small which struck as healer false crumpled to floor.

113

'Now changeling wounds should none have ever seen
but changeling rogue, by deeds, who law of gift did break.
Sensed I that king did warn of one unseen
nor sensed in land so hidden was. Now make
for feast do we, king leave in debt and slake
thirst mine,' did friend now laugh. 'Knew we that threat
had entered here,' did old man note. 'Mistake
made we but know not how this trap was set.'
'But now,' Dwarf shrugged, ' 'tis known why we in battle met.'

114

Man old, flat toned, advised guards two . 'Him place
where king is sure to find. Now we to feast
must go and thirst yours there will slake!' On face
of friend and dwarf did smile then break. Not ceased
did feel this quest since princes nine released
from life by northern king. Then bell did ring
to summon all to sit and share. In hall at feast
stools three not taken were. With thanks did sing
for life and food and friends' return then feast did bring.

115

As afternoon gave way to early eve
and feasting done did all to hall return.
Round council stone sat three from dreams, not leave
place this had they to feast. In vigil learn
did they of shroud whose secrets hid. Not seek to turn
did these as all round stone did stand to chant
then places take. Then friends, tale theirs, in turn
told they truth clear of journey made. No slant
did add to thrill nor stir, emotions too were scant.

116

As tale did end did all silent then stand
and speech of gratitude gave some,'Somehow
suspect do I,' with smile then nod and wave of hand,
'That time need you for rest,' to friends gave bow,
'for cards, doubts none, for pence to play as plough
does moon neath stars and thirsty you no doubt.'
So dwarf and friend did take leave theirs for now
to drink and play. Neath stars by fire did drought
on tongue relieve for chat and deal to start next bout.

117

Then eagle's cry in night pi'rced peace of theirs as dived
did mighty bird but land as changeling king.
'To pay debt mine must I do now. Contrived
does seem by fate, as bard in hall does sing.
But now to hall for three do I gifts bring.'
Then flowers grew round feet where king did stand
in tow'r of light too bright, for eyes. In ring
full bright shone he as solstice sun on land.
He entered hall, where silence fell, with gifts in hand

118

Then king, in east, alone stood now with gifts which bring
to hall had he. 'Receive from me friends three
this salt, wine red and bread for we soon sing.'
Then each these gifts partook of gratefully.
Of goddess born with radiant brow was he
who moved to hold and stand in mem'ried west
where bards reflect, so riven memory,
from mind is not, for mountain lakes lie blessed
by rain of seas which mem'ry treasured holds like chest.

119

Did hoary friend, mystical seer that left
for time windowed tow'r his, in north then stand
with staff. For time, not short, in life was he bereft
of mind as wild in forest hid and panned
night's skies to see what fates did hold in hand.
In north is solstice cold and short. Here rule
of winter reigns as sleep like death does land
on all. As these did move to place was stool
then placed by stone with chalice gold and water cool.

120

Then he from choir unceasing moved to south
and stood. Here fire and summer sun do reign
in golds and greens. Now chant did spring from mouth
of four, which none heard e'er before, to crane
in shroud as circle formed with hands. Did seem like grain
of sand in hand, this tune, as none could hold
in mind. Then four did cease as chant from plain
of one nigh tree, which ever blossoms bold
and red, did shroud undo so king could then unfold.

121
In silence cloak of crane was shown to all.
These four did each in turn, chant give, to weave
in cloak for Ahma's child gifts theirs so call
to them in dreams could do. For all perceive
could these in hall that knowledge to retrieve
of Aquila's and Ox too much for child
would be. For time did swirl and pass through cloak. Believe
did all and know of burden deep and wild
which child must face who slept in womb so warm and mild.

122
So cloak was gently placed in shroud with care.
Here hands unseen, re-wove and sewed. With silken thread
hands these then patterns merged and changed to share
and bind round cloak. Then bard in song all led
of parting's time, of oaths now kept as stead
fast true. In silence warm did four bless all
in hall. Depart did council then for bread
and rest as journeys fresh at dawn would call.
As embers died did dark of night them wrap like shawl.

123
Round stone in hall did four now vigil keep
o'er shroud and cloak. No fear, nor thought, of thief
this vigil birthed but brevity, till sleep,
where time unconscious of in life of men, like leaf
that forms and dies in seasons four. Like reef
in sailor's dreams do some death fear and strife.
Now all did sleep and dream in night so brief
till dawn rise would in misty haze and life
t'would seem return again where hopes and fears run rife.

124

'Dreams strange had I asleep in she who sleeps
in maze. Did feel that sand through fingers passed
too fast to hold or grasp. Each grain then keeps
its mem'ries deep of mountain thrust or blast
of molten stream e'en fallen star which fast
was held in earth once fall did break. Like sand in gale
these hist'ries known through mind did slip, so past
became like fleeting glimpse through breeze brushed veil
of naught, yet all, which in mind shadows cast so pale.'

125

'...And then did scape of dream slow change to dune
as mountain high, but sand, which e'en now grew.
This sand on dune not still did lie, to tune,
did dance, of wind and slope. Then slowly blew
through I a fear unable to subdue
for panic chaos then induced as sand
o'er head did close as sink in dune. Then rue
did I tune's spark till voice, 'Be still, mind yours command,
and master time.' This done, on dune did I then stand.'

126

'...And then did scape of dream return to where
in waters warm and safe slept I in dark
of womb as tomb in moonless night when glare
of midnight sun did golden hang and mark
did ripples make in waters warm where arc
of rainbow hung with em'rald tears that She
does weep for sorrows all. Did fade as hark
to mother's in and outward breath softly
called I to dreamless sleep and rest now peacefully.'

127
In morning's glow through mist did friends two rise
to see on cart now shroud was placed while steeds
on grass, nearby, did graze. In hall from ties
of vigil short were four, by dawn, shroud's needs
released therefrom to leave. 'Seems road now leads
to pool for time of rest till day ride we
for Ahma's maze through world of men where creeds
so broken were by princes nine. Foresee,
do I, a hope as some who creeds do keep still be.

128
'Moons two, fear I, is time so short dreams these
to grasp and hold till light see I on day
of birth. Not float do I in mother's seas,
constrained as I by womb now tight do lay
as arm or leg, through instinct's old, does flay
and strike. But still in waters dream do I
to beat of breath in drawn and out which play
and sing with drum of heart so slow ashere I lie
whilst heart of mine, so fast, infills with rythms high.'

129
' 'Twas warm in dream, in grove, as sun did set
on oak and ancient stone with gateways eight.
By way to west tall woman stood, who met
in dreams before have I. For me, did wait,
with open hand and smile by ancient gate.
Robe hers, hair long, e'en eyes, jet were. Not fearing stare
then I did look at open hand,' 'No fate
with fear e'er meet till met and weighed, with care,
on balance blind,' did mother warm, with me once, share.'

130

'In hand outstretched lay grains of corn unseen
before. In colours four a secret lies
well hid from mind of mine. Then lions green
and red by her did stand as fixed on stars were eyes
while corn placed she in hands of mine. Hard tries
mind mine scene strange to grasp as fade did she
with lions two. Then eyes to grain, then skies,
did flit to seek links missed in chain 'twixt me
and lions two as grove and grain could less now see.'

131

'To one in desert hid did glide in time
as question asked to some who watched as sat around
man old, 'If you a lofty tree would climb
then silent be in stillness sat. Not bound,
but unfettered, be free in thoughts. For found
for you a riddle old have I. If one
to self add I how many answers sound
would you? Know answers I from one so don
minds deep, which widely roam, to seek what in me shone.'

132

'As question lodged in mind no time to think
nor seek had I for tired in sleep became.
In mother's beat 'in breathe, out breathe' did sink
in rest as lab'rinth slept in mind. Lost name
did come and go, elude mind mine too tame
in tides of mother's sea and womb. From tomb
of womb arise will my dawn soon. Mind mine not lame
but peaceful sleeps,' From hall on harp, like loom,
did bard now weave tune soft to soothe child warm in womb.

133

To pool where dwarf and friend did watch and wait
did message come like owl which silent flies
in night. Tune wov'n by bard did pool placate
so Ahma's maze to them revealed could rise
in form full clear then fade, no ripple made. Now eyes
with mind did join in thought with actions none.
' 'Tis maze, but for us not. This lab'rinth lies
for mind of child, to solve, so breathe in sun
and cry first cry and we task have so can be done.'

134

On face of dwarf no grin did rise but swift
did stand and forehead slap. 'Forgot have I
of place in castle hid. See now that seek to lift
a veil must we on past unseen by eye,
unknown by all of us though old. When lie
did I when child, did know of place to seek.
An image hangs on wall in room, which try,
to grasp have I. 'Tis room, where thief not meek,
a queen became who nose of fate ne'er feared to tweak!'

135

Then friend and dwarf did enter room which doors had none.
On wall where image hung was opened door.
'So bored was she that riddle cracked for fun!'
laughed dwarf to friend as door closed he. Then saw
did dwarf why riddle solved, unsolved before.
For child with opened eyes at sun did stare.
'Of suns that shine through eyes, how many pour?'
Was riddle scrawled round child. Then dwarf with care
did eyelids close and push, ' 'tis two!' with friend did share.

136

Down stairs through opened doors with riddles solved went they
till one did reach where letter left. 'Had I
no time, as husband came, this door of grey
to solve. To me do write when need of eye
of thief have you!' With grin did dwarf now sigh
as letter wrote and hawk home sent. Now rest
and play at cards did dwarf and friend till cry
of hawk at gates did call for final test
of queen once thief. Nigh gates did dwarf now sense next quest.

137

As castle gate did open wide, where lay
pale lions two asleep, stood queen so old
with princess young. Then softly queen to dwarf did say,
'When young, of you, was I by mother told.
For queen knew you long now laid is with gold
in grave and I, 'tis clear, old am. But she
did tell of message you send would. Now bold
is daughter mine in art of thievery
untaught and message now makes sense to her and me.'

138

'For door of grey no symbols has,' grinned child
to dwarf with smile that he and friend knew well.
So four inside did talk of child once wild
and known by all till room did reach, 'Did tell
to us of puzzle room, lights none, pool dark and smell
of woods and trees outside within which grew.
When young was I did give, with wink, a shell,'
this princess grinned as shell did show as through
to pool did go doubts none, returned with water true.

139

When door of grey faced they did child then throw
pool's water cold round edges all. She bowed,
in breathed, out breathed on centre hard and low
in tone. Then pulse with breath did door. Not cowed
by sight unseen did she then scream so loud
with baby's cry which shattered door in way.
'To me grandmother once gave clue, 'o'er dead a shroud
like womb o'er babe does water soothe. Both grey,
when crying greet,' as shell did give to use this day.'

140

' 'Tis not for us to enter there,' did queen
to child with smile then say. To pool turned then did four
and amble slow. Here talked of times unseen
in lives of all so hist'ry's veil now tore.
Then questions answered were until no more
did rise from past so come had time to part.
Once dwarf, and friend, watched them slow leave, to door
returned to seek what hidden was. For start
of quest began in room. From there would they depart.

141

Now dwarf's thoughts turned to cart with cloak and shroud.
'Moon last for child in womb soon comes as dies
does one who fades above now us. Let cloud
in mind disperse and fade so see can we where lies
this quest. The cloak round child must be when cries
cry first, so live, not die if we, in time, there are,'
did friend now calmly state. 'Now he who tries
must now not fail,' words old did rise from far
in time known once in tale. 'Let thoughts not seeing mar.'

Flow

142

In mind of dwarf, did sight arise and trace
to place in world above. Dark nearby land
was feared by men. For lies did these embrace
from tales of lands of myst'ries strange where hand,
unseen, could strike and flay while beauty fanned
        the mind that lust did flaw. Then dwarf did roar
a laugh as friend on back did slap. 'Such sand
in mind! 'Tis here on hill which stands tall o'er
this castle larger in than out. Once blind. No More!'

(Faerie Kingdom under a hill; Robert Kirke etc)

143

In room on floor was mirror cold and black
in which reflections none of selves could see.
So dwarf, rod his, on glass did place but back
then took, surface not stired, when friend quickly
to cart did run, with shroud returned which he,
placed then, on mirror black. 'Tis bird grey's eye
which deep and slow, as flies, in which peer we.
        Record all seen do these for cranes to know. Not lie
do I for story old once knew. So I this try.'

144

Like moonless night did mirror dark now fade
and stairs revealed which downward above led.
    To pool did two retire and fire then made
to light up darkest night and sleep on bed
of grass and fern. Of tree, dreamed they, not dead,
that rose through stairs with lights to guide to hill.
Here midwife strange did wait for shroud. So still
were dreams as moonless night which stars with light sought fill.

145

'Does final moon seem swiftly born and rise
while mother stirs in sleep. Awake, not I,
nor sleeping am in visions clear to eyes
but mist to mind are these which swirl and fly,
elusive moths round light to dance. Though try
to catch through fingers slip do moths which flit
and spin, direction change e'er focus lie.
This lab'rinth mind, hard not to find does sit
like void, abyss, within, without, around, unlit.'

146

'In breathe, out breathe, now rest drifts mantra old
through clouds unknowing bright to light which flare
and die as rythm set as mother told
in dreams while slept. This teth does myst'ry share
as sense of serpent old whose breath seems bear
a lions strength subdued by fortitude
of flowered maiden kind but strong who lair
did find, subdue then lead with chain unpulled. So brood
did I so long but what links these does me elude.'

147

'When three arose in me in river deep
and breath quick relief took to lungs and heart,
was mind left river bound. Three states did seep
in creep. For on, above, below each part
distinct yet whole as one not three impart
a meaning clear to me e'en clue, 'cept mother, tune
conceived in me whose one in three. To start
from where do I this meaning seek? Tis soon
must deeper secret learn or die under this moon.'

148

'No tune from harp here calms nor stills from bard
unknown. Still mother's waters warm embrace
but less float I more rest on flesh not hard
but soft. Do sense slight pulsing new begins, a trace
from depths unknown which I in time must race
and lab'rinth solve or stillborn be and eyes
the light of sun ne'er see. Then eyes of grace
tears pure will weep for loss of chance and cries
as stairs remain unseen by I and fears will rise'

149

'Then all will brace themselves against a fear
return of kingdoms nine with sword and angry mind.
But superstitious fear becomes so clear
as nine will ne'er more rise. This fear will blind
or sheer, like blade or beast, the self maligned
it cripple can. Sense I this rhythm's change
does stronger grow to mother's breath aligned.
In breathe, out breathe, now rest. So mind now range
as rhythm grows and lab'rinth solve for now feel strange.'

150

'It comes friend old,' sensed dwarf, 'To stairs go we
to world of men in place fear they. There place
shall we this shroud and cloak. Midwife, maybe,
will us there meet. Stairs these unravel fate
and myst'ry hard. Moon's nine, in mind, create
old riddle deep. For thief, then queen, is dead
and yet when child born is, she's not. For time is straight
and simple not. *O'er us nine waves have spread
so queen is dead. For sun, nor moon ne'er here light shed.'

*(Concept of slower time in realm of Faery)

151

'In child is myst'ry reconciled of three.
For Ahma, born of queen from here and king
of men does two contain. But child, myst'ry
will be, for she born is of three. A thing
unseen now, silent, comes to all. Will bard then sing
and cloak reveal to child what now does weave
around and in if lab'rinth solved. So bring
to place must we this shroud and there not leave
till fate is seen and lab'rinth solved do I believe.'

152

'For stairs and tree do time relieve so wave
and moon be single phased. Stairs these untrod
before will we climb now for living child or grave.'
This dwarf did note in sombre tone as nod
to friend. Then each did slowly step where rod
light gave till stairs were gone. Then weavers three
in loom let dwarf and friend now flail as prod
did shuttle wild through stars with moons to free
the mind from wave and moon. Did seem eternity.

153

'In vision voice did come, relate, of myst'ry known
but grasp this not could I as womb did stir
and change so mind released did I for sown
was thought on riddle asked. If I confer
a self on self am four, yet two, does whir
not four, nor two but three. Does six exist
but answer not, for four in six infer
can I not do. In lab'rinth mine see twist.
Sev'n 'tis! Wake then will I if fifth by me is kissed.

(Solomon's seal: Quintessence)

154

'In visions lost a sleeper am, in sleeper lie
do I. Now feel do I this rhythm strong
increase.' In breathe, out breathe, and rest, don't try
just push. For sleeping Ahma restless lies
but watched over by maidens three whose eyes
speak naught. Their minds with midwife ride to hill
for shroud and cloak as weave do they time's ties
for dwarf and friend so three would meet. So still
had babe in womb become. Soon air lungs hers would fill.

155

Then dwarf and friend rise did through time to stand
once more in time once trod on hill. Alone
did midwife quiet wait. Here three spoke naught. As planned,
to midwife shrouded cloak was giv'n . Then shown
were dwarf and friend how call come would from throne
of she who'd suckle babe for time. Then time
did come and shroud was borne from sight. Intone
song old did she. Then three did weave the rhyme
of time on these so once again strange tree could climb.

156

When dwarf and friend emerged from room to pool
did go to rest for time till came the call
from throne. 'Think I the human sun is tool
to measure time, not moon. Then fate will fall
and call to child and she to stair guide we so all
can see the work of kingdoms nine undone.'
Did friend relate to dwarf with grin. From hall
of oak did tune of bard now fly and run
on wind, in streams 'cross lands and time, 'Ahma's begun.'

Flow

157

Now midwife sang and soothed Ahma's damp brow
with herbal water warm. Not wake would she
from sleeper's sleep till babe in arms somehow
would call for kiss as held nigh heart. Then free
would flow a mother's love and milk briefly.
Then Ahma's eyes once blessed with sight of child
would close in peace as sleep once more would call softly.
Now midwife softly chants with words so mild
which pulsing, pushing, pangs and pains midwife beguiled.

158

From distant market place did song untie
cranes shroud which babes' small strange and symbol'd robe
became
in midwife's hands as Ahma now a cry
let out. Then chant did change as candle flame
did light for coming babe. This chant, a name
so old, did whisper, pulse, like drum from heart.
In breathe, outbreathe and rest, again the same,
in breathe, outbreathe and rest and then restart
in breathe, outbreathe for now does babe from womb depart.

159

'Do feel now pushed through tunnel dark, so tight
yet warm. Through vision blurred here've been before
when old was I and darkness came, then light
did guide to waiting hands. But now is focus poor,
too much, too fast, I rest and wait. Yet sure
am I a phoenix cried as rose from ash.
Sense I now comes its birth afar once more
on mountain top in hidden land where flash
of light'ning hails its birth with mighty thunder's crash.

160

In hidden cave this babe was born and laid
on mother's breast. Then Ahma stirred at cry
and woke, kissed baby girl and smiled but made
no sound, nor name did speak. This babe did lie
and sleep in mother's arms for time. Nearby,
in stillness, midwife sat and watched did she o'er pair
who lay till milk did flow. Then lullaby
sang she for suckling babe. In time, with care,
did lift and robe this babe, then place on fur of bear.

161

As Ahma smiled, once more, on child of hers
and tune, the call to sleep and dreams did rise.
One final kiss gave she to babe who stirs
to stare, in Ahma's loving gaze, through eyes
not seeing clearly yet. As babe then lies
and stares does Ahma close eyes hers. Then light
from candle flickers slowly out and dies.
Now babe asleep does fall in crystal glow not bright
to tune of midwife's lullaby which sings of night.

162

In hall of oak does bard this lullaby
then weave so all in dreams would know of two
new born this day. Their future now did lie
in wasted land where naught did live. Now grew
a hope in darkest night of moon, and knew
did bard, a dawn would come for wasted land
where life again would rise. Till then imbue
the dreams of all would he, by tune from hand
on harp, with hope till two on wasted land do stand.

Afterword

'Grandad! That's not fair!'
'What isn't?'
'Well...what happens next, Who are the two?'
'What did the bard weave?'
'The bard told of two, probably the phoenix and the girl, in the shroud and cloak, go to the nine kingdoms and make everything better again and she sorts out the stair thing?'

'There you are, the story was finished in the bard's foretelling. Why does it matter that the 'How?' is not told?'
'It doesn't feel finished in the right way.'
'Is anything finished in the 'right way'? What does 'finished in the right way' mean? Let us imagine that the 'how' is told. What then? She is young, you would then ask,'What happened to her then and the dwarf and his friend, what of them?' So the story would never end because the story will never be finished in the 'right way'. That is, for many, the story of life.'
'Pardon?'
' Many feel that life does not end or unfold in the 'right way'. You could say that life sometimes doesn't happen or end in 'the right way'.

Grandad, that's a bit of a big jump from 'what happened?'
'Is it? Yes, I think it was too. But it's now there none the less.'

'Old Friends on the Mountain'

'Come friends,'
Taliesin, the silence broke.
'We three have lifetimes walked,
spirals ridden
and myst'ries seen.
'Have we not sat
at foot of mage and fool
in stillness,
to wisdom seek?
Now let us these learnings
share on mountainside,
'neath setting sun,
round autumn's fire
when veil is thin.

Blaise at Merlin smiled,
'Perhaps, to rest a while,
reflect
old friends, 'tis time.'

'Hmmm...'
Merlin so slowly pondered.
'Do opposites really exist?
If they do, how and why?'

The other two
into the fire stared
then three into cosmos pried
as spirals once lived,
again, they rode
and probed.

Flow

Then Blaise this silence broke,
'Come, let us, the art
of bardic mem'ry now employ
as thoughts take form
in spoken words. Let us
the patterns seek from random
lists of 'opposites'
which mutated have
from adjective to concrete noun
and human minds confused.
For sword of truth
the soul from spirit severs
but none ask,
'Why? How?' or
'What does that mean?'
So few this mystery explain.'

These three round fire then sat
and spoke in turn.
This list, which grew,
on patterned mem'ry they placed
like spread of cards
in canvas gypsy booth.

… Flow

                        good and evil

male and female   push and pull   right and wrong

                     choice and fate

nature and nurture   split and join

                      do and don't

live and die   wet and dry   low and high

                     sink and float

light and dark   hawk and dove   hate and love

                    hot and cold

scared and bold   coward and brave   white and black

                   long and short

fat and thin   here and not here

               betrayer and saviour

is and isn't   mortal and immortal   lost and found

               lazy and industrious

kind and mean   generous and miserly   swift and slow

               stillness and motion

full and empty   born and stillborn   brains and brawn

foolishness and wisdom   developed and undeveloped

                  untruth and truth

backwards and forwards   civilised and uncivilised

                  famine and plenty

                   all and nothing

                    Flow

                solid and liquid
fire and water   attract and repel
                knowledge and ignorance
rich and poor   have and have not
                married and single

prey and predator   wet and dry
                sacred and profane
belief and unbelief   trust and doubt

            And so their list
         and game of mem'ry grew
            till silence fell
          like cloak and words
              did cease.

           Now Merlin stirrred
              both flames
               and mind.
       'Of these let one be taken,
         scrutinised and sieved
         on which light can shine,
       illuminate and free the rest
    from concept's pointless ranting cave.
      The one which beguiled human minds
         and hid in conundrum false.'

   'On good and evil,' Taliesin posited swift
         and council of three agreed.

Flow

'In stillness be for time
must we for this in hand
with wisdom walks,' Blaise,
light toned, did note.' And there
let wisdom come, advise.'

'This conundrum, puzzle old was birthed by need
to understand,to judge, justify and explain.
But what is good or evil depends on
the position
of those that observe and judge
whether victim or dealer of deeds
in life.' Taliesin gravely noted.

'And here is where
conundrum's collapse comes.
When humans pose these thoughts and judgements bold
on the Divine their minds unwind and fear
will rise.
Flawed logic comes,' Blaise did add, 'If
the Divine is good
and evil exists,
then evil
created was,
by the divine.'

Merlin nodded and sighed.
'The paradox that 'exists not' except
in human mind. She, who anchored was,
was shown how 'all was good and all was loved.'*
My friend, Taliesin, now give form in words to your thoughts.'

(*Julian of Norwich)

Flow

'The mind
can take these 'opposites', adjectives,
and remould as absolutes
as rules and guides for behaviours and minds.
Here what is good or evil can be turned
and justified,
though horrified are those
on whom these absolutes do fall
or those who these observe.' Taliesin
sighed. 'But for mind to think
that it can then
judge the Divine as
humans can be judged?
That, is arrogance beyond.
Divine Good begat Divine Evil?
After all the Divine Good's
opposite must be Divine Evil?
Such thoughts does wisdom now undo
to show
Divine as beyond
our need for comparative adjectival opposites to understand
phenomena so we can tidily
store it.
The Divine is Good
and all created*
is good and loved.'

'So opposites
exist
in human minds alone
and then these they use as tools
to carve and understand
what cannot
be understood nor
explained,' Taliesin laughed.

(*Julian of Norwich)

Flow

These three
in jovial mood then
closed the veil
as sword did fall
and all in naught
in love
did
flow.

Canticle 1

Holy, Holy, Holy
is The Name.
The Name above, beyond, before and after
all names.
Holy, Holy, Holy
is the Unknowable, Inexpressable Name
above, beyond, before and after
all names.

All heartbeats of every living thing
cries Holy, Holy, Holy
is The Name
unnoticed, unfelt
by that in which the heart resides.

Holy, Holy, Holy
is the Name
rings even from the clickety clack, clickety clack
of travelling trains,
the underground,
the conveyor belts of industrial machines
which harm she that bore them with her minerals.

Holy, Holy, Holy is the Name
The Name above, beyond, before and after
all names.
Holy, Holy, Holy
is the Unknowable, Inexpressable Name
above, beyond, before and after
all names.

Canticle 2

At dawn, my Love
my heart sings of you
as night gives way to light.
It is the spring of this new day
to sing of You, to You.
I am born at dawn in Your spring
to sing to You, of You,
Your Love anew in me.

At midday, my Love
my heart sings of you
under your blazing noon day sun
It is the summer of this new day
to sing of You, to You.
I am maturing youth, working in Your summer
to sing to You, of You,
Your Love anew in me.

At sunset, my Love
my heart sings of you
as light gives way to dusk.
It is the autumn of this new day
to sing of You, to You.
I am older now, at rest in Your autumn
to sing to you, of you,
Your Love anew in me.

At night, my Love
my heart sings of you
as light gives way to night.
It is the winter of this new day
to sing of You, to You.
I now aged do die this night in winter
to sing to You, of You,
Your Love anew in me.

Canticle 3

Oh let all that lives, moves and is
cry Holy, Holy, Holy are You,
who is I Am.

Come raise your voice with mine
to pierce the cloud
which sits between Maker and made,
created and Uncreated,
born and Not born.

Oh let all that lives, moves and is
cry Holy, Holy, Holy are You,
who is I Am.

Come raise your voice with mine
to the Sun whose rays of Glory
always shine above this cloud,
this veil.
My soul would be like a pilot
who flies in full sun
beyond nature driven clouds.

Oh let all that lives, moves and is
cry Holy, Holy, Holy are You,
who is I Am.

Come raise your voice with mine
and honour, love and glory give
to the uncreated One who breathed us into
birth and She who wove
our formlessness into form.
Come sword of Truth now cleave
my soul free
so it can sing
of what Was, Is and will Be

Oh let all that lives, moves and is
cry Holy, Holy, Holy
are You, who is
I Am.

Canticle 4

Tonight I lie alone,
my Love.
My heart an empty bed
to which You haven't come
to hold me in Your everlasting arms
of peace.

Tonight I shiver cold
my Love.
My soul now naked lies
as You my blanket haven't come
to wrap nor warm in Your everlasting arms
of love.

Tonight I sleepless am
my Love.
My spirit tosses, strains its neck
as You my pillow haven't come
to raise my head and pillowed be
in Your everlasting arms
of bliss.

Tonight I pace
naked, cold as my mind
no rest will give with logic,
argument that I am now
unloved, abandoned, inadequate
for One so glorious.
Yet, my Love, though you don't come,
my heart and soul with spirit sing
of memories of you and your embrace
so soon this lullaby causes mind
to desist as sleep now comes.
Here I dream of You.

Canticle 5

As, in my shed doorway, I looked out
through soft autumn mizzle
Your sun warmed my naked arms as smoke
did twist and twirl
like prayers to You.

Then nasturtiums Your soft mizzle
with diamonds bedecked which glittered
in Your golden autumn sun.
Here silken threads, by spiders long abandoned,
did sunlight transform. Then dance did these in gentle breeze.
These golden threads did plant to old stone join
communicating dreams from seeds to mountain now long gone.

As whispering leaves caressed by Your gentle breath
sang songs to You of love and life
my heart joined in
and woke my soul from slumber deep.
Glory, Glory, Glory
sings all that lives
in our back yard
while traffic rumbles,
someone hoovers and others drill
and bang with hammers hard at work.

Flow

Doors open, muffled conversations rise and fall
to a backdrop of ringing phones.
But none can drown out these whispering songs
which rise to You. E'en the Faerie folk who tend these plants unseen
do pause and join this song of songs
to You in our backyard.
Oh You, with distaff
so busy in your weaving labour,
who sits and sings to all and all join in,
in our backyard,
Glory, Glory, Glory.

Then galvanised stairs ring their song
as child with parent jumps down everystep
rejoicing in the 'Bong, Bong' with giggles and laughter
as everything sings
Glory, Glory, Glory
in our backyard
in the autumn sun.

Canticle 6

My Love
I sat by the ocean today.
I thought of you.
The houses of people, behind me lay hidden in a mist.
I thought of You.
My soul leapt up, 'Come let us swim,
float, drown in the Love of our Lord and Love.
My mind and body...so divided.
Yet your Love called,
'Come, let My Love lift you up, enfold you.
My waters are warm, eternal.
Come My love come. Walk on these waters with Me.
I AM able to hold you, sustain you
by My Love alone.

Canticle 7

Our Lady comes
walking on oceans of love.
Fish rose as stepping stones singing
'Holy, Holy, Holy is
She who weaves, wove and will weave.'
As she stepped on to the shore
a smile,
a Tern went to Her hand.
'Fly my soul,' I cried,
'Fly to my Mother who wove me.
Take me to Her stars, Her waters, Her cave.
All hail my Mother who wove all into being
and will weave me out.
Holy, Holy, Holy.'

Canticle 8

No enemies assail Your gates.
Yet I release mine from within.
Fear, doubt flood my mind in the dark.
My own enemies assail me.
I run through the streets afraid,
seeking She who would calm.
I cry out in the dark.
I hear the 'Clickety-Clack'
but can't find You.
Mother,
are You hiding?
No, I know You are not.
I sense Your touch, Your voice.
I sit and sing to You,
Ave, Ave, Ave.
My heart leaps at thought of You.
Ave, Ave, Ave.
Blessed mother,
Holy Weaver.
You who felt Your heart pierced stll flow with love.
Ave, Ave, Ave
cries my heart and soul to you.
My enemies flee at my joy.
Ave, Ave, Ave.

Canticle 9

(Canticles of the birds)

'Little Wren, little Wren, who did you see, who did you see?'
'I saw Oram, deep in his grave.'
'What did he say, little Wren, what did he say?'
'He sang,' 'Glory, Glory, Glory,' 'a thousand times.
Then we sang Holy, Holy, Holy a thousand times'
'What did He say little Wren, what did he say?'
'He sang,'
'Fear not life, nor death, neither heaven nor hell
for Love is all and all is Love,
Glory, Glory, Glory

Canticle 10

(Canticles of the birds)

'Little Cock Sparrow, little Cock Sparrow,
who did you see, who did you see?'
'I saw Mother Julian asleep and at peace
where her anchor held firm.'
'What did she say little Cock Sparrow, what did she say?'
'She sang,' 'Ave, Ave, Ave,' a thousand times
and then we sang Glory, Glory, Glory.'
'And what did she say Little Cock Sparrow, what did she say?'
'She sang,' 'Fear not, for all is good and all is loved.
So fear not life nor death, neither heaven nor hell
for all will be well for all is loved.
Holy, Holy, Holy.'

Canticle 11

(Canticles of the birds; Druid Dubh (bh- ve) - Blackbird)

'Druid Dubh, Druid Dubh who did you see, who did you see?'
'I saw an old man hidden in his towering cave'
'What did he say Druid Dubh, what did he say?'
'He sang, 'beware, beware, beware a thousand times.'
'And then we sang Oh people,
Oh People, Oh people a thousand times.'
'What did he say Druid Dubh, what did he say?'
'He sang,' 'beware the quest that becomes the prize
not what was once sought.
Beware the gnat.
Beware the untamed tongue which burns down forests.'

Canticle 12

(Canticles of the birds)

'Old Owl, Old Owl who did you see?'
'I saw a little weeping man in grey dancing with joy.'
'What did he say Old Owl, what did he say?'
'He who taught us birds to sing Joy to the world
sang,' 'Love, Love, Love.'
'Then we sang Glory, Glory, Glory a thousand times.'
What did he say Old Owl, what did he say?'
'He sang,' 'dance for Our Lady, juggle for Our Lady,
so Her joy fills Our Lord.
Glory, Glory, Glory.'
'And then we sang,'
'My Love, My Love, Glory, Glory, Glory,'
'a thousand times.'

Canticle 13

(Canticles of the birds)

'Oh Heron Grey, Oh Heron Grey who did you see,
Who did your see?'
'I saw a wounded king asleep in a bower of stone
with scabbard empty as sword returned to She.'
'Oh Heron Grey what did he say, what did he say?'
'He sang,' 'Two streams, two streams forever flow, forever flow.'
'And the we sang, Christi, Corpus Christi a thousand times.'
'What did he say, oh Heron Grey, what did he say?'
'He sang how all, in time, would be so well.
Love, Love, Love. Then we sang
Christi, Corpus Christi a thousand times.'

Canticle 14

(Canticles of the birds)

Oh Lettered Crane, Oh Lettered Crane what did you see,
what did you see?
'I saw innocents slain that one might live.'
Oh Lettered Crane, oh Lettered Crane
what did they say, what did they say?'
'They sang,'
'Oh foolish kings and rulers,'
'a thousand times then,'
'Oh fools who slay with no thought nor care,'
'a thousand times.'
'What did they say, oh Lettered Crane, what did they say?'
'They sang,'
'No justice, No justice,'
'a thousand times.'
'Then we sang, Glory to the Guiltless who too was slain,
a thousand times. then,
Glory, Glory, Glory to the Lamb
a thousand times.

Canticle 15

(Canticles of the birds)

Oh Eagle Mighty, Eagle Mighty what did you see,
what did you see?'
'I saw she of ebony skin, robe of blue and distaffs two.'
'What did she say oh Eagle Mighty, what did she say?'
'She sang,' 'My heart was pierced in love
a thousand times, a thousand times.'
'And then she sang,' 'My beloved Child,' 'a thousand times.'
'What did she say oh Eagle Mighty, what did she say?'
'She sang,'
'Rejoice all mothers,'
'a thousand times.'
'Then we sang,' 'The Bridegroom, My Child
comes for His Bride,' 'a thousand times.'

Canticle 16

(Canticles of the birds)

'Oh Phoenix Flaming, Phoenix Flaming what did you see,
what did you see?'
'I flew to Mighty Aquila, the Queen of birds in cave in void.
We flew to where all and nothing
breathes in and out.'
What was said, oh Phoenix Flaming, what was said?'
'The Unknowable sang,'
'Be still and know on inward breath, Be still and know
on outward breath,' 'an infinite times.'
'What was said oh Phoenix Flaming, what was said?'
'As a million stars were born and died we sang,
Be still and know, Be still and know.'

Canticle 17

(Canticles of the birds)

'Oh Glorious Flock, Oh Glorious Flock what will you sing,
what will you sing?'
'At dawn we sing Joy to the World.
At noon we silent weep for all.
At sunset we sing a thousand times
Joy to the world
When all do sleep
we a vigil keep.'

Canticle 18

(Canticle of Mary Magdalene, the most loved of all)

My Love did kiss me on the mouth.
His breath I shared.
My breath He shared.
Ten breaths we shared.
I breathed in His Love and He breathed in mine
as I lay naked on His breast.
We breathed creation pure.
My Love my Desire
We breathed the base of all.
We breathed and shared such Splendour.
My Love, my Desire.
We breathed Victory.
My Love my Life.
We breathed and shared all Beauty
My Love, My Lord.
We breathed in and breathed out Justice True.
My Love, my Love.
We breathed and shared
such loving, Merciful Kindness.
My Love, my Balance.
We breathed in, breathed out
such Understanding.
My Love, my Love.
We breathed in Wisdom's arms.
My Love, my Love.
Then Cosmos ceased,
Shekinah came within the veil
and All was and was Not.
I knew not whether I was my Love or my Love was me.

Then angry men did push aside the twelve true
and all was gone.
They stripped off me my Lord's robes.
They washed away His oils and balms
and cast me naked to the rabble
who laughed, poked and jeered.
I had no shame but
'Prostitute'
was proclaimed.
Soon dirt stained
and in rags I, as beggar, walked.
My Love, my Love
I'm True, I'm True.
I stole behind their sacred veil to await my Love.
But far away in pain was He.
When lightning flashed,
the veil was torn,
I wept
exposed.

Near a garden tomb I walked.
Two heartbeats in me in time did beat.
Then someone came,
the veil did tear.
My Love, My Desire, My Lord and King.
Forever now Your Shekinah
through me
will shine.

Canticle 19

(Lament of the Magi)

Oh people, Oh people
we three were neither wise nor kings.
Falsehoods abound.
For we were Magi,
readers of stars and portents
but not listeners to the voice behind the sign.
So arrogant were we.
We knew the sign and what it meant
but foolish we caused slaughter of innocents.
A King of Kings,
so we did think,
to a king would be born.
For we served kings, pharoahs,
mighty temples.
So to Herod went.

Oh yes,
his the deed but ours the blame.
The shepherds on the hills were wiser
than we.
They saw the sign and wondered at its meaning.
Oh people, Oh people
if only we too had wondered.
For Angels came to poor shepherds
and the message clearly gave.

Oh yes, we found the king
and gave our gifts
even opened to the Voice so to Herod
did not return.
But three hundred cry out to us,
'Wise? Wise? Wise?'
No, we answer, not we,
not we.

INDEX TO POEMS

	Acknowledgments	i
1	Foreword to Chalice	3
2	10 Thoughts	Pg 5
3	On …..	Pg 14
4	Against	Pg20
5	Doubt	Pg 21
6	On Internal Strife and when to Ground oneself	Pg 22
7	In the Void	Pg 25
8	In Darkness	Pg 27
9	On Being Equal	Pg 28
10	The Will in Service	Pg29
11	Why?	Pg 31
12	What's in all this for me?	Pg 32
13	On Psychic Protection	Pg38
14	On Rigidity of Thought and Action	Pg39
15	I don't believe in anything so why light a Candle?	Pg48
16	Streams of Blood and Tears	Pg51
17	Gist	Pg57

Limited notes on Origin & Ahma's Labyrinthine Child

These notes don't cover the entire poems. They cover the salient symbolism which then is repeated through the poems

1)
Aquila: Paracelsus: Queen of birds and philsophers of alchemy.
Shadowed Sky: The Cave in Plato's Republic 514a – 520a
Cranes: Many myths ascribe cranes as the origins of alphabets, guardians of the underworld and the form Apollo took to escape Typhon. Theseus's escape from the labyrinth influenced the Crane Dances' or maze dances.
Being still in nothing is well described in WG Gray's Living the Tree. The naught is also the Ain of this tree, the nothing surrounding the unkowable crative being of force behind the universe.

2)
Drawn from countless creation myths and The Western Tree of Life. Blood and Water flowing from a single source in context of the solar system derives, here, from the writings of Paracelsus.

3)
A tongue in cheek response to 'The God Delusion' by Richard Dawkins.

4)
Within the nought on tree is the Ain Soph or limitless infinity here represented as number swithout start of end.

5)
The Ox: From 'Reproof of the bards' where Gwion/Taliesin notes that he alone knows the name on the Ox's headband, a mystery known only to those entitled to the bard's secrets which is linked to, again, the spiral or maze.
The link to 'The Plough' star system is a poetically licensed leap.

6)
This is drawn from the concept of the 'Music of the Spheres' on which many have written since the times of Pythagoras so is not expanded here except to say that Allegri's Misere is a good example of someone who has tapped into the concept.

7)
Dew and rain/mist: Rosicrucian terms for light of sun and moon.

8)
The concept of order arising but still vulnerable and subject to chaos.

9 to 18)
The birth of the microcosm.
The reference to Light is the Ain Soph Aur which is the limitless light which surrounds the creative unknowable from which and to flows all.

10 & 11)
The lesser lights. This again has drawn on the writings of Paracelsus and the Rosicrucians where the light of moon is the lesser light but the foundation of the spiritual journey to union with the all and none as the first phase of balance of masculine and feminine with humans. Madame Porette was burnt at the stake for calling this annihilation which with mystical richness of the book was a tragedy.

13 & 14)
The crow / raven is one of the alchemical symbols for the first steps in alchemical process for transforming self which is the colour of the black residue from the first process or steps to the philosopher's gold or stone. The birds which then appear in order represent the completion of the process.

16)
Using different waters(salt, crystal)was also a part of the process.

Notes
Ahma's Labyrinthine Child

1 – 18)
These stanza's were inspired by Dante's Inferno and Puck of Pook's Hill. Here the shades of those who once lived don't talk with the dwarf or friend in order to emphasise the seemingly incalculable age of some of the poem's main characters which continues the themes of the prelude.
The choice of characters and trades relate in part to the Republic where Socrates and others debate what type of people would a utopian state allow to reside in it.
The first three (vs 1 -6) are cast as individuals whereas the last 6 (vs 7 – 18) are representatives of their group.

11)
Four stringed lyre is a reference to Pythagoras's music of the monochord relating to the 1st, 4th, 5th and major 6th.

13-18)
The nine kingdoms' structures collapse to create a wasteland reminiscent of TS Eliot. Allegorically the concept of the bursting of the west's 5% bubble in a world where 95% can't afford £5 on a book each month and houses are still made of mud, canvas or corrugated tin but is driven by an atheistic scientism where religion (Not for all obviously) is controlled or at worst not tolerated or fundamentally destructive under the guise of democracy or dictatorship.

16)
The cost of the human made pompeii where the acts of men produce the same effects as a volcano.

17)
A worldwide concept of the souls at death reaching a river and needing a spirit bridge to cross over. Also it maintains the western tradition from Pythagoras, through Plato, the Bible, Dante and Milton etc.

19)
Scientia rom latin Scire- to know. This verse reflects the change from Pythagorian and Platonic thought to Aristotlian. An example in the renaissance the battle between Keppler and Fludd where they debate over whether quantative methodology is superior to qualitative.

20)
Bath is a reference to Archimedes. Gentle folk is used here as a generic term for faerie, sprites, nymphs etc.

22)
Teth: The moon in the Jewish Cabbalah. The first step beyond living to die. Also linked to Leo and the tale biting serpent.

23)
A play on' fell at first fence', see prelude Book 1.

24)
The aspect of choice of narrow / wide path in life was first promulgated by Pythagoras and the symbol accreditied to him.

25)
Nine Sorrows: Drawn from the Novena of Our Lady of Sorrows celebrated 7th – 15th September. This maps the nine sorrows of Mary. What follows here is the classic lament which appears in oral traditions and later most written texts on suffering of many.

31)
Hoary: Old way of describing those with white hair symbolising that they were close to winter and death. The concept of the elders sitting at village gates to which people went for advice.

32)
Silver pearl tears as healing inspired by Elizabeth Goodge.

37)
Hence the fate of the anciet mariner.

40)
Taliesin, Merlin and Blaise.

155) Goddess in mother form feeding babe with Divine milk

After this most themes and symbols can be worked out from Chalice and the first story.

ABOUT THE AUTHOR

Paul lives, writes, paints, tells stories and sings in Mid Wales.

Made in the USA
San Bernardino, CA
26 February 2017